THE GLOBAL ECONOMIC CRISIS

AND POTENTIAL IMPLICATIONS FOR FOREIGN POLICY AND NATIONAL SECURITY

FOREWORD BY
JOSEPH S. NYE & BRENT SCOWCROFT

EDITED BY
NICHOLAS BURNS & JONATHON PRICE

The Aspen Institute
One Dupont Circle, N.W.
Suite 700
Washington, DC 20036

Published in the United States of America in 2009 by The Aspen Institute

Design by: Steve Johnson

aspen strategy group

Acknowledgements

Nicholas Burns
Director, Aspen Strategy Group

Jonathon Price
Associate Director, Aspen Strategy Group

In early August 2009, the Aspen Strategy Group convened for a week in Aspen, Colorado to measure the effects of the global economic crisis and examine its implications on U.S. foreign policy and national security. This book is a collection of the essays that were commissioned for the summer workshop; it includes the nine papers used to guide our discussions, flanked by a scene setter and a set of concluding observations.

As always, the Aspen Strategy Group is grateful for the support and dedication of many groups and individuals. Without their support, the summer workshop— and the book you are now reading—would not have been possible. We would like to thank the Margot & Thomas Pritzker Family Foundation, the Feldman Family Foundation, the Markle Foundation, the Bill & Melinda Gates Foundation, the Resnick Family Foundation, Booz Allen Hamilton, and Exxon Mobil for their support. We would also like to thank Howard E. Cox, Simon S. Pinniger, Thomas O'Gara, Terry Turkat, Leah Zell Wanger, and William E. Mayer for their generosity and dedication to the Strategy Group.

As the Obama administration nears the end of its first year in office, we would like to congratulate several of our former ASG members who are now serving at senior levels in the administration. First and foremost, we would like to congratulate former ASG director Kurt M. Campbell on his appointment as assistant secretary of state for East Asian and Pacific affairs. We know Kurt will bring the same understanding and deep knowledge of foreign policy and national security to the Department of State that served the ASG so well. As former public servants, we understand the challenges Kurt and our friends and colleagues face, and wish them luck as they navigate through this increasingly turbulent chapter of American and global history.

Additionally, we would like to thank our General Brent Scowcroft Award fellows, Alicen Bartle, Marshall Lilly, and Sarah Golkar for their inexhaustible work ethic and ubiquitous optimism in pursuit of this endeavor—a promising indication of bright futures to come. Rebecca Weissburg provided her excellent proofreading and editing skills throughout, for which we are deeply grateful.

Finally, our deepest gratitude and highest regards go to our co-chairmen, Joseph Nye and Brent Scowcroft; it is under their guidance that ASG thrives and sustains these vital dialogues, ensuring a meaningful debate on the implications of this Great Recession. Their leadership facilitates ASG's legacy as a forum for bipartisan inquiry, dialogue, and ideas.

Contents

Part **1**
HISTORICAL PERSPECTIVES AND CURRENT CONDITIONS

Part **2**
PREDICTIONS ON THE COURSE AND EXTENT OF THE GLOBAL ECONOMIC
CRISIS AND ITS LARGER IMPLICATIONS

Part 3

ARE INSTITUTIONS READY FOR THE CHALLENGE?

Part 4

CONSEQUENCES FOR DEVELOPMENT AND DEMOCRACY

Part 5

CONCLUDING OBSERVATIONS

Foreword
by ASG Co-Chairmen

Joseph S. Nye, Jr.
ASG Co-Chairman

Brent Scowcroft
ASG Co-Chairman

As a group that primarily considers the national security issues confronting the country, the topic of the global economic crisis posed a unique challenge for the ASG. When the group was forged over twenty-five years ago, familiar challenges included arms control, a menacing Soviet Union, and the threat of nuclear war. Rarely—if ever—did the group worry about issues such as budget deficits, trade imbalances, and corporate bankruptcies. However, as the extent of the economic crisis crystallized in the fall of 2008, policy problems began to appear that fell in both the realm of economics and national security. For example, following the collapse of Iceland's currency and stock market, Icelanders took to the streets to demand—and eventually receive—the government's resignation. And in at least some corners of the globe, the Washington consensus of open markets and limited government was declared dead and a new Beijing model of greater government involvement in business was welcomed. Some leaders proclaimed that the financial crisis represented the beginning of the end of American power.

Though it is too soon to tell whether these changes are permanent shifts or merely rash reactions to the economic events of the last year, they deserve greater analysis. Therefore, to better understand the nexus of the economic system and its impact on America's national security, the ASG invited leading economists to join our annual summer workshop and broaden our understanding of the complexities this crisis could present.

Such is the immensity of the problem that after five days of thought-provoking discussion, the group was still uncertain of the degree to which this economic crisis represented a fundamental shift in the balance of power around the globe. Some seemed to think it might; others remained skeptical. However, the sessions illuminated the myriad of impacts already underway and reinforced the need to think through and prepare for future challenges that remain over the horizon, even perhaps restructuring the American institutions constructed at the end of World War II in order to prepare for a changing and increasingly interconnected world.

How the United States reacts to the global financial crisis will have repercussions for decades to come. The effects of this crisis would be consequential even if they were only limited to the domestic realm, but with two unresolved wars, a surging China, and a recalcitrant Iran and North Korea, the intersection between the financial crisis and national security must be better understood as the U.S. seeks to maintain its position as a global leader. This summer workshop provided the ASG with the opportunity to discuss bipartisan strategies for addressing a crisis which knows no party lines and demands a unified and coherent response.

The ASG, with its diverse membership from across party lines, is uniquely suited for this analysis. Conceived as a bipartisan policy forum during the Cold War, the Group has evolved over the years, moving beyond the framework of the Cold War and into the realm of transnational and multifaceted issues that blur the lines between international and domestic issues.

As during the Cold War, the U.S. has a distinctive role to play in this crisis. As the world's dominant economic force, it must lead by example and reinvigorate the global economic recovery. If it can rise to this challenge, chances are good the U.S. and its economic system will emerge strengthened, both domestically and on the international stage. To move forward, this crisis will have to serve as a wake-up call to the United States to reform the flaws in its system, and more effectively utilize whole-of-government solutions. However, if the U.S. fails to correct its course or allows the world to perceive that America is unable to respond adequately to this crisis, it could call into question America's ability to solve other global problems and the resulting long-term effects could be even more serious than we think. Over the last twelve months, the United States has made several decisions that appear to have put the U.S. back on stable footing, but the key policy choices to remain on this path are in front of us, and we hope this volume will help the government focus on how to steer through the rough roads ahead.

Preface
by Aspen Strategy Group Director

Nicholas Burns
Director, Aspen Strategy Group
Professor of the Practice of Diplomacy and International Politics
Harvard University

Each year, Aspen Strategy Group members and experts devote the summer session to an in-depth study and discussion of a dominant issue that is at the heart of the current international agenda. It thus wasn't difficult to choose our 2009 topic—the global economic crisis and its impact on U.S. national security.

On the final day of our 2008 session, one of our members, Phil Zelikow, warned that the challenges posed to the U.S. by the leading international political and security issues would pale in comparison to a world economic crisis. Others cautioned this was a critical moment to reexamine the international financial architecture, which was under severe strain and headed for collapse. Five weeks later, in mid-September, we all watched as the global economy, which had grown so impressively during the preceding decade, imploded, plunging the world into a Great Recession that still dominates the international landscape.

This 2009 Aspen Strategy Group study looks at the origins of the crisis and what history can teach us in order to cope with its many challenges. It also focuses on the ability of the U.S. and other leading powers to sustain successful diplomatic, military, economic, and development policies in the year ahead.

In addition to our group members, we assembled an impressive group of economists and business leaders to examine the impact of the economic crisis on the Obama administration. We focused on whether the United States can remain the supreme global political and military power at a time when our economic influence and leadership have never been more questioned by the rest of the world.

Since his election to the presidency in November 2008, President Obama has made clear that stabilizing international financial markets, restoring consumer confidence, and preparing the way for an eventual recovery are his most critical responsibilities as president and leader of the world's largest and most important economy. His early efforts to produce an aggressive $787 billion stimulus bill, pass a historic budget, and restructure key industries while tackling health care and climate change have been extraordinarily ambitious in their scope.

It remains to be seen, however, whether the current weakness of the American economy will lead to a decline in the ability of the U.S. to exercise power in the more traditional domains of diplomacy and military affairs. President Obama has acted correctly, in my view, to broaden our efforts in Afghanistan and to return the U.S. to a leading role in the Israeli-Palestinian negotiations. He has committed the U.S. to a potentially fateful diplomatic engagement with Iran and has tried to reset and restore stability to our relations with Russia.

But, will President Obama be able to convince the Congress and average Americans to pay the costs of such a vigorous leadership role at a time of economic decline and anxieties at home? We will look closely at whether the huge financial costs of the economic crisis will inhibit a continued, lead American diplomatic engagement in the world.

For many of the administration's stated policy goals, securing the necessary resources from Congress is absolutely critical. Yet along Pennsylvania Avenue, divisions are emerging between those who argue that more spending is—and will be—necessary to put America back on track and others who contend we must be concerned with the mounting deficits and seek to restrain future spending. How will this widening divide affect the administration's mandate and ability to act? Will future and historic budget deficits permit the expansion of the American Foreign Service and the rebuilding of a broken USAID, which we concluded at last summer's workshop were critically required? Will the U.S. be able to sustain large development programs such as PEPFAR at a time when developing countries are among the hardest hit by the global downturn? Will Congress concur with expensive and long-term military engagements such as the one President Obama may be suggesting for the U.S. in Afghanistan?

On Capitol Hill, how will the public mood affect Congress and their support for free trade agreements with important U.S. allies and partners such as South Korea and Colombia? As bailout fatigue settles in and Wall Street banks begin to repay money from TARP, will Congress agree to expand significantly the ability of Treasury and the Federal Reserve to play a much more vigorous international role, as they clearly must, given the dimensions of the current crisis?

Another important question for the Obama administration is this: Will it now change the way Washington has traditionally worked by placing economic issues on a par with the military and diplomacy when calculating the national interest?

In February, Director of National Intelligence Dennis Blair warned Congress that the global economic crisis is now "the primary near-term security concern" for the U.S. But when the Obama administration announced early on that "Defense, Diplomacy and Development" would be the core of its foreign policy agenda, the logical question arose—how about economics? Isn't America's international economic position now the most important indicator of our national strength? Shouldn't economics now be at the core of our foreign policy?

In this book, we examine the consequences of the economic crisis that is still unfolding and the national security and foreign policy implications for American power and America's role in the world. Here is a summary of the issues and questions we should keep in mind as we address the scale and impact of the economic meltdown on our nation.

Historical Perspectives and Current Conditions

We will examine the root causes of the current crisis and what we might learn from the past century's history of economic crises and their aftermath. Some have compared the current crisis to the Great Depression, others have termed it the Great Recession, and still others say the future remains uncertain. We will seek to discern the key similarities—and differences—between past periods of economic downturn and today's climate. We asked Martin Feldstein and David Leonhardt to help us think through the economic history of the last seventy years since the Great Depression to understand the prescriptions that have been used in the past and could be applied today.

Predictions on the Course and Extent of the Global Economic Crisis and its Larger Implications

We will consider the course and extent of the crisis and its implications for U.S. national security and global leadership. From the more tangible threats arising from instability in already fragile states to the intangible and long-term threats emanating from Chinese and Russian challenges to American global leadership, there are a myriad of over-the-horizon national security concerns produced by the current crisis. Richard Cooper, Bruce Stokes, and Laura Tyson analyze how the crisis has affected American allies and rivals alike, and what this new global landscape means for U.S. security, trade, budgets, and strategic interests. We consider how Washington can respond to the security concerns that have arisen from the economic troubles and how and where it may need to adjust its approach to respond to the changed environment.

Are Institutions Ready for the Challenge?

We look at the strength, capacity, and capability of international and domestic institutions to cope with the crisis. It is widely recognized that the current economic crisis is but one of many global challenges that will require international cooperation. Future policymaking will be anchored in our ability to balance the demands of a complex and interconnected global system with the realities of national politics. Kemal Derviş and David McCormick focus on the challenges, both near- and long-term, which face the United States and international coordinating bodies as they try to cope with and manage the current crisis. There is a long list of suggestions to restructure the system in order to be better equipped for the challenges of the 21st century. Specifically, we focus on the configuration of the G-20 and its rising prominence on the world stage. We also examine the Bretton Woods Institutions and think through how to retool domestic and international economic bodies to streamline policymaking.

Consequences for Development and Democracy

We also discuss the potential fallout from the financial crisis on international development and democracy. Sylvia Mathews Burwell and Mike Green focus on the changing face of development and how to balance the difficult challenges of maintaining international development commitments when domestic economies are floundering. Additionally, we focus on the impact the economic crisis has had on democratic norms and governance, and the power shifts in the international system, paying particular attention to China and its increasing importance as a key player in the international economic system.

Policy Recommendations and the Economic Outlook

Finally, we look to the future to arrive at some shared assessments of the challenges facing the U.S. as a result of the economic crisis. We seek a way forward to promote U.S. national security interests. And, we try to peer over the horizon to determine the financial future the U.S. will face when it emerges from this crisis.

Part 1

HISTORICAL PERSPECTIVES AND
CURRENT CONDITIONS

"In retrospect, the great irony of the economic policies of the Roosevelt administration was that the isolationist focus on domestic issues postponed the very policies of military assistance and U.S. mobilization that eventually brought the United States to a full recovery."

—MARTIN FELDSTEIN

Economic Conditions and U.S. National Security in the 1930s and Today

Martin Feldstein
Professor of Economics
Harvard University

In his annual report to Congress, the new director of national intelligence identified the global economic crisis as the primary current threat to U.S. national security. He focused on the risk that falling incomes and rising unemployment in emerging market economies could destabilize those countries politically, a reminder of how the global economic downturn in the 1930s contributed to the rise of the Nazis in Germany and the fascists in Italy.

His surprising focus on an economic issue also understandably raised interest in the more general subject of the relation between economic conditions and U.S. national security. The organizers of this Aspen Strategy Group meeting have asked me to comment on the experience of the U.S. economy in the 1930s, its lessons for managing the current economic downturn, and the relation of U.S. economic conditions to our future national security.

The current economic downturn is the most severe recession since the 1930s, already longer than any of the eleven previous postwar recessions and likely to involve a substantially greater loss of GDP. It is more damaging and more difficult to end because its basic cause was different from that of previous recessions. Those downturns occurred after the Federal Reserve raised the real short-term interest rate to deal with an inflation problem. When the Fed concluded that the higher interest rate had slowed the economy sufficiently to deal with inflation, it reversed its policy and lowered the rate of interest enough to end the downturn.

In contrast, the current downturn was caused by a general underpricing of risk in financial markets and in other asset markets, leading to an excessive rise in leverage. While the defaults on subprime mortgages gave the first warning that this was about to end, the need to reprice assets was much more general.

Unwinding the high leverage and the mispriced risk has left us with a financial system that remains dysfunctional and that is therefore not providing the credit that the economy needs for economic growth.

But despite these unusual problems, the current downturn is, as of now, far less severe than the depression of the 1930s. Even the most pessimistic forecasters are not expecting a repeat of that experience. The level of real GDP has declined about 5 percent since this recession began. In contrast, real GDP fell 10 percent in the first year of the recession that began in 1929 and eventually declined more than 30 percent before it began a long, slow recovery. The unemployment rate is now approaching 10 percent, but rose to 25 percent in the 1930s despite a large number of public employment programs. Current systems of unemployment insurance, Social Security, and Medicaid mean that there is far less personal hardship than there was in the 1930s.

The current situation also differs from the 1930s in several other specific ways that reduce the risk that today's economy will deteriorate into a major depression. I will note just three of them. First, in the 1930s, banks were the primary source of credit, while now the capital markets and various nonbank institutions play major roles in credit creation. Second, federal government insurance of bank deposits means that a bank failure no longer destroys the wealth of the depositors and the fear of bank failures no longer leads to bank runs, as it did in the 1930s. Third, the expansion of federal government spending since the 1930s provides a large, stable component of aggregate national demand.

Against these favorable conditions is one important negative difference since the 1930s. Because financial wealth was much more concentrated in the 1930s than it is today, the collapse of the stock market had a direct effect on many fewer households than it does in today's economy, characterized by 401k plans and IRAs. Nevertheless, unless our economic policies are very badly managed in the coming year, we will not slide into a downturn of the scale of the 1930s.

U.S. Economic Experience in the 1930s

One reason for optimism about current economic policies is that professional thinking about economic policy is very different today than it was in the 1930s. Policy officials should therefore be able to avoid the mistakes that turned the recession that began in August 1929 into the Great Depression.

Thanks to the work of John Maynard Keynes and Milton Friedman, we now have a better understanding of how governments can (at least in principle) reduce the severity of major economic downturns. Keynesian economics taught us that government spending can raise GDP and reduce unemployment. Friedman's work taught us that temporary tax cuts and transfers that temporarily raise personal incomes are relatively ineffective (unless they change the incentive to spend) while permanent tax increases (even if their starting date is delayed) will depress current spending.

Friedman's analysis of monetary policy in the depression also taught us that maintaining or expanding the "money supply" (i.e., the volume of currency and bank deposits) is important for sustaining and growing aggregate demand. The contraction of the money supply in the 1930s was particularly damaging because the supply of bank money was also the basis for the supply of credit to businesses and households.

Because these lessons were not known in the 1930s, the depression lasted longer and was deeper than it could otherwise have been. The Federal Reserve actually reduced the money supply by 30 percent between 1928 and 1933. The Roosevelt administration flailed around with a variety of counterproductive microeconomic policies (the NRA, WPA, CCC, Wagner Act, etc.). The scope for expansionary fiscal policy was very limited. Since federal government spending was only 3.4 percent of GDP in 1930, even the 40 percent rise in nominal federal government spending that resulted from the various Roosevelt spending programs was only equivalent to 2 percent of GDP.

There was also little room for a permanent tax cut since federal tax revenue was only 4 percent of GDP. Quite remarkably, the government actually doubled tax rates on high-income individuals between 1929 and 1932 and then raised them further in 1936. The only successful macroeconomic policy was the result of temporarily leaving the gold standard in 1933 and then returning to it at a higher price of gold the following year, an action that automatically caused an increase in the money supply. The unemployment rate remained at more than 17 percent as late as 1939 and declined substantially only when the government began a serious military buildup after the U.S. formally entered the war on the Axis powers in 1941.

Current Macroeconomic Policies

Friedman's lessons about the importance of money and credit helped to shape Fed policies in the current downturn. In addition, the Federal Reserve and the Treasury have acted forcefully in an attempt to extend credit in the economy. In addition to policies to help the banks, they supported credit through money market mutual funds, commercial paper, Fannie Mae and Freddie Mac mortgages, and even various consumer loans. But the banks have restricted their lending because the rising rate of defaults on mortgages and other loans creates uncertainty about the value of their existing assets and therefore of their capital. The Treasury's Troubled Asset Relief Program (TARP) and the more recent Public Private Investment Partnerships (PPIP) are attempts to resolve the banks' problems, but, for a variety of reasons, they have not been successful in removing the toxic assets from the banks' balance sheets. It is not clear whether the administration and Congress will agree on the steps needed to fix the PPIP program in a way that will lead to a recovery of bank lending.

The Obama administration recognized the need for a Keynesian fiscal stimulus, but underestimated the amount of stimulus and the speed of action that was needed to offset the combined effect of reduced consumer outlays and the fall in residential investment. Because of the specific design of the stimulus package, it delivered relatively little increase in GDP per dollar of increased national debt.

From 2009 to 2011, only about 25 percent of the increased national debt will come from an increase in federal government purchases of goods and services. The remaining 75 percent will come from reductions in taxes and increases in transfers to households or state and local governments. Consumers have responded to transfers and temporary cuts in taxes by saving most of the resulting increase in income. For example, the most recent rise in personal income of $180 billion between April and May 2009 led to a rise in consumer spending of only $25 billion, with the rest going to pay debts or accumulate financial assets. Likewise, a substantial portion of the transfers to states will be saved or used to finance spending that would otherwise have been financed with available revenues.

In short, although the basic conceptual lessons that followed from the experience of the 1930s caused a fundamental qualitative shift in monetary and fiscal policies, the magnitude of the government's actions has not been adequate to the problems that we now face. The fiscal stimulus will cause a temporary reduction in the rate of economic decline in the second and third quarters of 2009, but is unlikely to do enough to initiate a sustained expansion this year. Without knowing what new policies will be adopted, it is impossible to know when a sustained recovery will actually begin.

International Issues: Trade and the Dollar

International trade and exchange rates are controversial issues in the best of times, but can become a source of serious conflict when the economy is weak. Trade conflicts can, at a minimum, make it difficult to achieve cooperation on other international security policies. Although we are now likely to avoid the blatant protectionist policies of the 1930s and the resulting reciprocal tariff wars, some of the policies that are now being considered could have the same effect of creating trade conflicts. It is therefore worth understanding what happened in the 1930s and where similar trade conflict risks lie in current policies. Likewise, the value of the dollar and its role as a reserve currency has already become a source of friction between the United States and China. The administration has yet to enunciate a policy in response to its critics and is pursuing domestic policies that could exacerbate this issue. This section looks first at the trade issues and then at the current exchange rate problem.

The centerpiece of America's international trade policy in the 1930s was the Smoot-Hawley Tariff Act, enacted in 1930 to reduce imports by causing American firms and households to shift their purchases to American-made goods. Because the tariff rates were tied to physical volumes of imports (e.g., $1.12 per ton of pig iron), the sharp fall in the U.S. price level (down 29 percent from 1929 to 1932) caused the implied effective tariff rate to rise rapidly. While the Smoot-Hawley bill initially only raised the already high average tariff rate from 38 percent to 41 percent at the time of passage, the decline in the price level eventually caused the average tariff rate to rise to 60 percent.

The passage of Smoot-Hawley hurt the exports of foreign countries. That led to retaliatory increases in foreign tariffs that reduced U.S. exports by more than producers gained from the "buy American" effect of the Smoot-Hawley tariff. Fortunately, since international trade was then only a small part of the U.S. economy, the depressing effect on economic activity was also relatively small. The net exports of the United States fell by less than 1 percent of GDP. But the passage of the Smoot-Hawley tariff not only depressed U.S. economic activity, it also reinforced a sense of economic nationalism among our trading partners and led them to conclude that the U.S. did not care about their economic hardship.

Although the post-war tradition of GATT rules and WTO conventions will probably prevent a repeat of the 1930s style unapologetically protectionist tariffs, there is a danger that some of the recent U.S. policies and proposed future policies will lead to harmful reductions in trade and to increases in trade conflict. The "Buy American" provision of the recent fiscal stimulus act requires that all products paid for by the stimulus funds be made in America unless doing so would violate international agreements. In practice, state and local governments and others using stimulus funds have focused on the injunction to buy American, inducing retaliation and threats of retaliation by foreign governments and firms. This is likely to become a much bigger problem as the volume of purchases funded by the stimulus package grows.

The administration's cap and trade policy for reducing CO_2 emissions may, if enacted, lead to a more serious problem of explicit tariff increases and retaliation by foreign governments. Any cap and trade policy would raise the prices of American-made CO_2-intensive consumer goods. Those higher prices would put American products at a competitive disadvantage relative to similar goods produced in other countries. If the cap and trade policy becomes law, American firms will ask for "border adjustment" tariff increases and export subsidies to achieve what they will call a "more level playing field."

Surprisingly, WTO officials have already said that such tariffs and subsidies could be WTO compatible, perhaps by analogy with VAT border adjustments. But the product-by-product price increases caused by cap and trade would be vastly more difficult to estimate than the impact of value added taxes, especially in a system like the one proposed in the Waxman-Markey bill, with permit giveaways and a wide range of allowable purchased "offsets." The legislation would therefore create ample opportunities for all firms to claim protection and export assistance and for foreign governments to argue that all such adjustments were inappropriately large. This could cause significant trade friction with our trading partners, especially with China, India, and other emerging market countries that will not impose similar cap and trade policies or other comparable carbon taxes.

Such trade frictions would make it more difficult to achieve cooperation on other aspects of economic policy, especially security related trade policies like the imposition of tariffs and embargoes on a country like Iran.

A declining dollar could be a further source of economic conflict and political disagreement between the United States and other countries. The real trade weighted value of the dollar fell by 25 percent between 2002 and 2008, primarily because of the enormous U.S. trade deficit. Since then it has risen by about 13 percent, leaving a net decline since 2002 of 15 percent. The rise of the dollar since early 2008 reflects the desire of American and foreign investors to hold dollars because of the extreme uncertainty caused by the financial crisis.

As economic conditions stabilize, portfolio investors in the United States and elsewhere—including governments and non-government investors—are likely to want to shift more of their foreign exchange from dollars to other currencies. Recent comments by senior officials in Russia, China, and India—all major holders of dollars—indicate that such portfolio shifts may occur in the next few years.

A fall in the value of the dollar relative to other currencies is a natural and necessary response to massive trade imbalances. A lower dollar will make American products more attractive in foreign markets and American goods and services relatively more attractive in the United States. But if this occurs at a time of economic weakness abroad, the rise in imports of U.S. products and the fall in exports to the United States could lead foreign governments to adopt policies to restrict U.S. imports and promote foreign exports. That, in turn, could lead to increased conflicts over trade policy.

Foreign governments with large dollar investments are understandably nervous about the value of the dollar. Although their criticisms are about the role of the dollar as a reserve currency, the dollar investments of the Chinese and other major holders of dollars are far greater than traditional reserve balances. These are major forms of national investment, whether held in sovereign wealth funds or other accounts.

The legitimate concern of the Chinese, for example, is not about the future exchange rate between the dollar and the Chinese yuan, but about the future purchasing power of the dollar; that is, about future inflation in the United States. They worry that the massive U.S. budget deficits and the explosion of reserves at the commercial banks could lead to future inflation that makes their dollars buy fewer American goods.

If they act on these worries, they will shift more of their foreign exchange investments from dollars to other currencies. That would lower the value of the dollar and increase U.S. inflation. It would also cause long-term U.S. interest rates to rise, reducing the value of bonds and hurting the U.S. economic recovery. It is not clear what retaliatory policies the United States might contemplate under those circumstances, but foreign investors may fear a modern-day equivalent of closing the gold window to deny foreign investors free access to sell their dollar balances.

A policy that would reassure foreign investors of the future purchasing value of their dollar assets would involve reducing future fiscal deficits and making clear that the Federal Reserve will prevent domestic inflation even if that requires raising interest rates during the early stage of the recovery, when unemployment rates are still quite high.

U.S. Economic Conditions and National Security Issues in the 1930s

The Hoover and Roosevelt administrations were so focused on domestic economic weakness until the late 1930s that they essentially ignored the deteriorating security conditions in Europe and in the Far East that would eventually drag the United States into war with Germany, Italy, and Japan. In retrospect, the great irony of the economic policies of the Roosevelt administration was that the isolationist focus on domestic issues postponed the very policies of military assistance and U.S. mobilization that eventually brought the United States to a full recovery.

Economic considerations conditioned the way the U.S. reacted to specific foreign events. The United States did nothing substantive to respond to the aggressive actions of Germany in central and eastern Europe, of Italy in Ethiopia, and of Japan in China. While the U.S. protested the Japanese invasion of Manchuria, it muted its protests because of the importance of U.S.-Japan trade. The U.S. refused to admit Jewish refugees from Hitler's Germany because of (or rationalized by) concern about the impact of immigrants on the employment of Americans at a time of very high unemployment.

The isolationist sentiment in the United States and the decision to focus on the domestic economy led to the Neutrality Acts of 1935, 1936, and 1937 that restricted the sale of munitions to any of the belligerents. This effectively helped Germany and Japan because they had the domestic manufacturing capacity that Britain, France, and China lacked.

Budget deficits were a political constraint on military expenditures, reinforcing the political desire to belittle the risks to the United States of the events on the other sides of the two oceans. The federal budget shifted from a small surplus in 1930 ($800 million, or 0.8 percent of GDP) to a deficit of $2.8 billion, or 4 percent of GDP just two years later. The primary reason for the deficit was the drop in tax revenue caused by the economic downturn. Nominal GDP fell by one-third between 1930 and 1932, causing federal tax revenue to decline from $4.1 billion in 1930 (4.2 percent of GDP) to less than half that amount in 1932 ($1.9 billion, or 2.8 percent of the reduced GDP). This revenue decline occurred despite—or perhaps partly because of—a doubling of the income tax rates: The top tax rate, on incomes over $1 million, rose from 25 percent in 1929 to 63 percent in 1932; the rate at $100,000 rose from 25 percent to 56 percent; and even at an income of $10,000 the marginal tax rate rose from 6 percent to 10 percent.

Despite the foreboding events in Europe and Asia, U.S. military spending began to rise only after 1936—and the increase was slow until war was declared in 1941. Spending on the Army and Navy (there was no Air Force until after World War II) actually fell from $831 million in 1931, or 1.1 percent of GDP, to $705 million in 1934, also about 1.1 percent of GDP. Even as late as 1939, the combined Army and Navy outlays totaled just $1.4 billion, or 1.5 percent of GDP. But mobilization was underway in 1941, raising Army-Navy spending to $6.3 billion, or 5 percent of GDP, four times the 1939 level. And by 1943, Army-Navy spending had increased another ten-fold to $63.3 billion or 32 percent of GDP.

The rise in military spending created the demand that pulled the economy out of the depression. The Keynesian "multiplier" process meant that the total rise in GDP was more than enough to finance the increased Army and Navy budgets. By 1943, the nonmilitary GDP had increased to $136 billion, nearly 50 percent higher than in 1939. Even after adjusting for the price level increase, the real nonmilitary spending had increased by 14 percent.

U.S. Economics and National Security Today

The current national security situation of the United States is, of course, fundamentally different from the one we faced seventy-five years ago. Yet there is a risk that we will again underestimate the dangers abroad and therefore devote too little of our GDP to military spending and other forms of national security. And as in the 1930s, national security spending today could actually stimulate overall economic activity.

With the collapse of the Soviet Union, the U.S. nuclear umbrella no longer induces the kind of cooperation and support for U.S. policies among our traditional allies that it did in the earlier postwar decades. We are now part of a multipolar world in which the European Union, Japan, China, and Russia are independent actors pursuing their own national interests.

The Chinese are rapidly becoming a global economic power and potentially a global military power. Although China's per capita income is still low by Western standards, China's population of 1.3 billion people is more than four times that of the United States. If China's annual rate of real aggregate GDP growth continues to exceed that of the U.S. by just five percentage points (less than the gap in recent years), China's total real GDP (now nearly $8 trillion at purchasing power parity prices) will exceed that of the U.S. by 2025. While China's per capita income will still be relatively low, its large total GDP will allow it to support military and foreign policy activities comparable to those of the U.S. and Europe. By devoting a larger share of its national income to these activities, China would be able to do so even sooner than 2025.

The financial crisis has amplified the voices of those who criticize capitalism in general and globalization (free trade and capital movements), in particular. The very visible success of the Chinese economy and the destructive effects of IMF policies in Asia and Latin America in the late 1990s have called into question the "Washington Consensus" guidelines for emerging market economies. There is a further danger, as the DNI's testimony earlier this year indicated, that the declining levels of income and employment in emerging market economies could destabilize the political regimes in those countries. Political actors like Hugo Chavez and Mahmoud Ahmadinejad are using their oil resource income to support governments and nongovernment groups working against U.S. interests. American spending on foreign assistance, on helping our natural allies, and on supporting programs that strengthen market economies could help to counter those threats.

Another source of risk to the United States is our position as a major international debtor, dependent on other countries to finance our large annual current account deficit and continually roll over our vast outstanding international debt. Foreign investment in the United States (including foreign ownership of U.S. businesses as well as portfolio investments in U.S. equities and bonds) is now more than $20 trillion and exceeds U.S. investments in the rest of the world by more than $3 trillion. The additional 2009 current account deficit (the sum of the trade deficit and the net investment payments owed to foreign investors) that needs to be financed by foreign governments and foreign private investors is running at about $400 billion and is likely to rise in response to the recent increase in the price of oil.

Although we will inevitably attract foreign funds to finance the additional borrowing as long as we have a current account deficit, the risk is that foreign investors will be willing to provide those funds only at higher interest rates. A rise in interest rates caused by reduced foreign demand for U.S. securities would depress U.S. economic activity in the short run and economic growth over the longer term. The best way to reduce this dependence is to cut our long-term fiscal deficits by limiting the projected growth of government spending.

A further source of U.S. dependence on other countries is the increase in the relative volume of oil imports. Oil imports, as a share of total U.S. oil consumption, have risen from about 15 percent in 1955 and 40 percent in 1975 to 65 percent today. The suppliers of that oil are not reliable allies. Since it is clear that we will not significantly reduce our dependence on oil imports any time soon, we must have the naval and other military capabilities to be able to protect our access to that oil in the Middle East and the shipping of that oil in international waters.

The military threats facing the United States have also become more complex and more worrisome because of changes in technology and in the nature of our adversaries. In the 1930s we felt well protected by the distance of the United States from potential adversaries in Europe and Asia. The Soviet development of intercontinental ballistic missiles changed that after World War II. Today we face not only nuclear weapons but also biological and chemical weapons of mass destruction. We are only beginning to understand the potential destruction that could be caused by cyber attacks.

We now face three different kinds of adversaries. There are the traditional major powers (Russia and China) that could attack the United States with conventional or nuclear weapons. An increasing number of rogue states and regional powers (including North Korea, Iran, and potentially Pakistan) are developing similar capabilities. Non-state terrorist actors like al-Qaeda could acquire and deliver a nuclear weapon or other weapon of mass destruction. All three types of adversaries have or could develop the ability to use cyber attacks against U.S. interests.

Despite the massive increase in threats to the United States, we have reduced our commitment to defense spending. The share of GDP devoted to defense declined from 9.1 percent in 1960 to 4.9 percent in 1980. After a temporary rise under

President Reagan (to 6.2 percent of GDP), defense spending fell to 4.9 percent of GDP in 2008 (including the spending on the wars in Iraq and Afghanistan.)

The recent budget submitted to Congress by the administration significantly reduces the GDP share devoted to defense over the next decade. Defense outlays are projected by the administration to decline from 4.9 percent of GDP to 3.8 percent in 2019. In real terms, defense spending would rise less than 1 percent a year.

The failure to support a more robust defense is a matter of political choice rather than economic necessity. The growth of the entitlement programs (i.e., of the so-called "mandatory programs") and the unwillingness to raise the tax share of GDP have together forced a large reduction in the share of GDP available for defense. More specifically, total federal tax revenue was 19.7 percent of GDP in 1969 and is projected in the Obama budget to remain nearly the same (20.3 percent) in 2019. During the same half-century, the mandatory entitlement programs rose from 5.6 percent of GDP in 1969 to 11.2 percent of GDP this year and are projected to increase to 13.2 percent in 2019. The 7.6 percent of GDP increase in entitlements between 1969 and 2019 will come primarily from reduced defense spending, projected to be down by 5.3 percent of GDP.[1]

The share of GDP spent on defense could be increased permanently without cutting entitlements or raising marginal tax rates by reducing some of the special "tax expenditure" features of the federal income tax. For example, eliminating the current exclusion of employer payments for health insurance would raise more than $100 billion a year in additional revenue, an amount equal to about 0.8 percent of current GDP and more than 20 percent of defense spending.

The decision to include virtually no defense spending in the stimulus package (only $13 billion of the $787 billion stimulus bill) reflected the political resistance to increasing defense outlays. I suggested in a *Wall Street Journal* article that a temporary surge in defense outlays would be an effective way to stimulate GDP in the current situation.[2] That article led to discussions with each of the four service chiefs who confirmed that, as a result of several years of conflict in Iraq and Afghanistan, they had equipment that needed to be repaired and supplies and equipment that needed to be replaced. Such spending would not raise the defense budget baseline, but would simply bring forward in time the spending that would eventually have to be done.

The military leaders with whom I spoke also indicated that they could do substantial infrastructure spending on their bases in the United States. Such outlays could begin immediately because they would not need the kinds of local approvals that are required for civilian construction projects.

The defense services could also increase recruiting, training new recruits with civilian skills and returning them to the private economy at the end of two or three years. Although these temporary recruits would not have performed useful military work during that time, they would have had valuable education and would be available as future members of the armed forces reserves.

I was surprised to learn that the services had been told by transition team members and later by the new White House officials that because the recession had reduced national income they would have to cut back their military spending. This, of course, has the economic logic exactly backward. Because of the economic weakness, a temporary rise in military spending would not require cutting back on other forms of public and private spending. It made no economic sense to tell the services that they had to cut back while the government was searching for other ways to spend money as part of the stimulus package.

But increasing military spending alone will not fully defend the United States against its increasingly sophisticated enemies. The recent decision to establish a new Cybercommand is a clear recognition of the risks of cyber attacks as well as of cyber-based military and industrial espionage. Foreign governments and government related actors use cyber espionage to steal military and industrial secrets. These governments or their agents have also planted bugs in the systems of U.S. public utilities (including the electric grid, city water systems, and transportation control systems) that could allow them to cause those systems to malfunction or to stop functioning entirely. Unfortunately, the ability of the Cybercommand and of the Department of Homeland Security to develop a robust defense against cyber espionage and cyber attacks is being restrained by concerns about the invasion of privacy. Now that the cyber risks are explicitly recognized, there are likely to be substantial national security and economic benefits to working with other nations to develop ways of preventing a dangerous escalation of cyber attacks.

Finally there is the problem of preventing organized terrorist activity in the United States, including future events like the 9/11 attacks. Substantial progress has been made in recent years to shift the mandate of the FBI from its traditional crime fighting role to a broader one that emphasizes counterterrorism. Changing the culture of an organization like the FBI is, of course, very difficult, and some of its rules, procedures, and organizational structures are still more suited to crime fighting than to counterterrorism. Although some of the legal restrictions on FBI activities have been modified to allow it to be more effective in counterterrorism, the FBI is still restricted in ways that do not hinder the British MI5. Moreover, the FBI budget process and the magnitude of its resources have not expanded in line with its increased responsibilities.

A Concluding Comment

While it is difficult to summarize the complex economic and national security lessons of the 1930s, several points seem clear.

1) Although the current recession will be long and very damaging, it is not likely to deteriorate into conditions similar to the Great Depression of the 1930s. Policymakers now understand better than they did in the 1930s what needs to be done and what needs to be avoided.

2) The focus on domestic economic policies in the 1930s and the desire to remain militarily neutral delayed the major military buildup that eventually achieved economic recovery. The administration's current budget points to a one-fifth reduction in the share of GDP devoted to defense over the next decade. In light of the increased range of adversaries and threats that the nation now faces, there are likely to be substantial national security benefits to increasing the share of GDP devoted to defense and other aspects of international security.

3) A well-functioning system of bank lending is necessary for economic expansion. We have yet to achieve that in the current situation.

4) Raising taxes, even future taxes, can depress economic activity. The administration's current budget proposes to raise tax rates on higher income individuals, dividends and capital gains, corporate profits, and all consumers through the cap and trade system of implicit CO_2 taxes.

5) Inappropriate trade policies and domestic policies that affect the exchange rate can hurt our allies, leading to conflicts that spill over from economics to impair national security cooperation. Reducing long-term U.S. fiscal

deficits would reduce the likelihood of future inflation and thereby reduce the fear among foreign investors that their dollar investments will lose their purchasing power.

6) The possibilities of domestic terrorism and cyber attacks create risks that did not exist in the 1930s, or even in more recent decades. The scale and funding of the FBI and the Department of Homeland Security is not consistent with these new risks.

Martin Feldstein is the George F. Baker Professor of Economics at Harvard University and President Emeritus of the National Bureau of Economic Research (NBER). In 2009, President Obama appointed him to be a member of the President's Economic Recovery Advisory Board. Previously, he served as President and CEO of the NBER from 1984 to 2008 and 1977 to 1982. He continues as a Research Associate of the NBER. In 2006, President Bush appointed him to be a member of the President's Foreign Intelligence Advisory Board. He served as President of the American Economic Association in 2004. From 1982 through 1984, Martin Feldstein was Chairman of the Council of Economic Advisers and President Reagan's chief economic adviser. Dr. Feldstein is a Director of the Council on Foreign Relations and a member of the Trilateral Commission, the Group of 30, the American Academy of Arts and Sciences, and the Council of Academic Advisors of the American Enterprise Institute. He has been a director of several public corporations and is currently a director of Eli Lilly. Dr. Feldstein earned a B.A. from Harvard and a B. Litt, M.A., and a D. Phil. from Oxford University.

[1] The remaining 2.3 percent of GDP increase in entitlements and the 1.7 percent of GDP rise in interest on the national debt are balanced by the increase in the fiscal deficit (up from a surplus of 0.3 percent of GDP in 1969 to the administration's projected deficit of 4.4 percent of GDP in 2019).

[2] Martin Feldstein, "Defense Spending Would Be Great Stimulus," *Wall Street Journal*, 24 December 2008.

"Of course, economic growth—wealth—is also a crucial source of global power. And there is nothing inevitable about the United States remaining the wealthiest country in the world."

—DAVID LEONHARDT

Pulling Back from the Crisis:
A Roadmap for the Future of the American Economy

David Leonhardt
Economics Columnist
The New York Times

Bubbles are a useful metaphor. But they also have a flaw. Real bubbles—the kind that children blow in the backyard—pop. Then they are gone forever. Financial bubbles, on the other hand, deflate, sometimes slowly and sometimes quickly. In many cases, they deflate a little, inflate again later, and ultimately deflate some more. Like the backyard kind, financial bubbles eventually disappear. But the process can be messy.

The United States economy—like the global economy—is now suffering the after-effects of two giant bubbles. The first is a stock market bubble that has been around much longer than many people realize. It began to inflate in the mid-1980s, deflated during the 1987 "Black Monday" crash and then, starting in the early 1990s, began inflating again for nearly a decade.

It's easy to think of the turmoil of the past two years as being unconnected to the stock bubble of the 1990s, which appeared to end with the dot-com crash of 2000 and 2001. But, dramatic though it was, that crash did not come close to erasing the excesses of the 1990s. Indeed, in many ways, Wall Street after the crash looked a lot more like it was in a bubble than a bust.

Arguably the best track record for measuring the stock market is the long-term price-earnings ratio. Based on the past ten years of corporate earnings to smooth out the swings in profits created by the business cycle, it is the measure favored by the economist Robert Shiller. Over the past century, this ratio has averaged roughly 16. At the peaks of the dot-com bubble, it exceeded 36. At its recent nadir, in 2003, it remained above 20. By 2007, it was back above 26—higher than at any point since the 1930s. Quietly, the bubble had returned.

And this time, there was a second bubble, too. For decades, and maybe longer, house prices had risen roughly with incomes. If prices rose a little faster for a few years, they soon slowed down—or, in certain regions, even fell—and incomes caught up. But starting in 2000, the relationship broke down. Based on the economic fundamentals, houses appeared to be overvalued by somewhere between 20 and 40 percent.

These twin bubbles were caused in large measure by an explosion of debt and, in turn, fed that debt explosion. Loans had become easier to get, be it for investment banks or families, and borrowers used those loans to buy assets, bidding up the price of those assets. The continuing increase in the price of these assets then made households, financial firms, and others feel flush. So they became willing to borrow more and save less. Wall Street took on ever more leverage, setting aside ever fewer assets. The household savings rate fell close to zero. But the boom in asset prices had raised families' and firms' net worth, making the decline in savings seem not to matter. In 2001, Lehman Brothers—of all places—published a report entitled, "Are U.S. Households Saving Too Much?"

Over the past two years, we have begun the process of unwinding these debts. Economists refer to the process as "deleveraging." It isn't much fun. To repay their debts, businesses cut their costs, including their workforce. Sometimes, they go bankrupt. Households reduce their spending, loans are harder to come by, and the economy enters a deep recession.

By the spring of 2009, the worst of the financial crisis appeared to be over, thanks in large measure to aggressive policy responses from the Federal Reserve, the Treasury Department, and foreign governments. But the worst of its impact is almost certainly not over. As Carmen Reinhart and Kenneth Rogoff recently wrote, "the aftermath of banking crises is associated with profound declines in output and employment."[1]

Indeed, there are likely to be times over the next year when the economy will seem as if it may never recover. The unemployment rate, already at its highest level in a quarter-century, has further to rise. Foreclosures will continue to mount. The credit markets may yet have more surprises ahead—and so may the stock market. As of mid-July, the market's long-term price-earnings ratio was just above 16—or roughly equal to the average of the past century. This was up from a recent low of 13. But in the wake of the other two great bear markets of the last century, in the 1930s and early 1980s, the ratio fell to 6 at its nadir—years after the crisis had begun, in both cases. The economic risks, as a forecaster would say, appear to be to the downside.

Even if the economy avoids those downside risks, it still will not feel very good to most Americans for some time. For one thing, the economic expansion that ended in 2007 wasn't very good to most families. It is the only sustained expansion on record—going back to World War II—in which median family income did not set a new record high. As a result, many families will be making little more in 2010, accounting for inflation, than they were a full decade earlier.

This stagnation is likely to have political ramifications. We need look back to only the early 1990s to imagine what those ramifications might be. Then, a recession—and a relatively mild one at that—ended in the spring of 1991. But the economy still felt weak enough in November 1992, twenty months later, that voters turned a once-popular wartime president out of office. Two years later, with job growth and income growth still mediocre, economic anxiety was a contributing factor in the Democrats' November 1994 loss of the House of Representatives for the first time in four decades. And as late as 1996—a year that we now remember as being part of the go-go late 1990s—Pat Buchanan won the Republican New Hampshire primary while referring to his supporters as "peasants with pitchforks." That same year, *The New York Times* ran a series on "The Downsizing of America" and *Newsweek* ran a cover story on chief executives who were laying off large numbers of workers. The headline was "Corporate Killers."

All of this is to say that large parts of the next eighteen months could end up being dominated by the short-term condition of the economy. A midterm election looms in 2010. Congress and President Obama may decide that more stimulus is needed. The Federal Reserve and the Treasury Department will need to remain vigilant about the condition of the financial system.

This attention will, by and large, be appropriate. The main policy error of past financial crises has been timidity. Japan, when dealing with its long slump, cut government spending even as it was announcing new stimulus packages. Franklin D. Roosevelt flirted with fiscal discipline midway through the New Deal, and the American economy paid the price with the vicious downturn of 1937. Today's policymakers—Ben Bernanke, Henry Paulson and Timothy Geithner—made a similar misjudgment last year, allowing Lehman Brothers to collapse. Vigilance is the strategy endorsed by history.

Yet history serves up another lesson, as well: This too shall pass. As Larry Summers said in a speech this March at the Brookings Institution: "Our problems were not made in a day, or a month or a year, and they will not be solved quickly. But there is one enduring lesson in the history of financial crises: they all end."[2]

The real uncertainty, then, is not whether the American economy will escape its current slump; it's what will happen once that slump ends. What will the economy of the future look like? Above all, how fast will it grow?

Economic growth can seem like an abstract concept. There is a cliché that posits, "You can't eat GDP." Yet, the consequences of a country's growth rate are not abstract at all. Slow growth makes almost all problems worse. Fast growth helps solve them. As Paul Romer, the Stanford University economist and renowned expert on growth, has said, the choices that determine a country's growth rate "dwarf all other economic-policy concerns."[3]

Growth is the only way to pay off the government's debts in a relatively quick and painless fashion (through rising tax revenues without rising tax rates). This is precisely what happened in the 1950s and 1960s to pay off America's World War II debts. Growth expands the size of the nation's economic pie, making it far more likely that American workers will receive healthy raises in the future. And growth will make it easier to pay off the enormous looming bill for the baby boomers' retirement, especially their medical care.

Thanks to an annual growth rate of 8 percent, average income in China has quadrupled in the last two decades and living standards have soared. An affluent, industrialized country like ours cannot grow at 8 percent. But even seemingly small differences in annual economic growth can matter enormously because of the power of multiplication.

Shortly after the Civil War, the average person in the United States was still substantially poorer than the average resident of England. Over the century that followed, this country's per capita growth rate was only about half a percentage point a year faster than England's—which was still enough to make Americans significantly richer than the British and turn this country into the world's dominant power. If, over the next two decades, growth could be lifted by just three-tenths of a percentage point, it would completely pay for the $770 billion stimulus package. So, it turns out you can eat GDP—as well as use it to heat yourself, cure yourself, educate yourself, pay your country's debts, and build the world's strongest military.

Unfortunately, there are real reasons to worry about the long-term growth potential of the United States. From the early 1970s through the early 1990s, American economic growth was alarmingly slow—slow enough to create a mini-industry of books envying the German and Japanese economies. Then the 1990s technology boom made those worries disappear. But in the last few years growth has slowed again, close to its disappointing levels of the 1970s and 1980s. The tech boom no longer seems certain to fuel decades of rapid growth, as the industrial inventions of the early twentieth century did.

Growth in the current decade, even before 2008 and 2009 made their dismal contributions, has averaged 2.5 percent a year, significantly slower than in any decade since the 1930s. That's worth repeating: Even before the Great Recession took hold, annual economic growth in the current decade was slower than it had been in the 1940s, 1950s, 1960s, 1970s, 1980s, or 1990s. And the fraternity of growth experts in the economics profession, like Robert Gordon at Northwestern and Dale Jorgensen at Harvard, predicts that, on its current path, the economy will grow more slowly in the next two decades than it did over the last two.

If the United States cannot reverse this growth slowdown, the implications are clearly serious. The country's enormous debts will be harder to pay off. Its military obligations will be more difficult to maintain. The living standards of the population will grow at a frustratingly slow pace. And the country's international influence will, in all likelihood, ebb.

For centuries, people have worried that economic growth had limits—that the only way for one group to prosper was at the expense of another. The pessimists, from Malthus and the Luddites on, have been proved wrong again and again. Growth is not finite. But it is also not inevitable: It requires a strategy.

Economists—the good ones, anyway—don't pretend to know precisely what causes economic growth. Demographics are obviously one factor. Arithmetically, economic growth is simply the product of hours worked and productivity, and a more rapidly growing population allows for faster growth in hours worked. In an aging society, immigration—especially the immigration of highly skilled, productive workers—is one of the surest ways to lift growth. Beyond demographics, though, economic growth is something of a black box.

The best-known strategy for lifting growth over the past generation has been tax cuts. And the theoretical argument for the connection between tax cuts and economic growth is a solid one. When tax rates are lower, people have more incentive to work. Their added efforts will accelerate growth. The question, however, is the magnitude of these effects. Are tax rates the main force that drives growth? Or are they a relatively minor factor, given all the other forces affecting an economy?

The empirical evidence from the past half-century is surprisingly strong on this matter: Taxes do not seem to be nearly as important as we might think. When, over the past sixty years, did the American economy grow fastest? In the 1950s and

1960s, when the top marginal tax rate was a now-unthinkable 90 percent. What is the only period over the past generation when the economy nearly matched the performance of the 1950s and 1960s? The late 1990s, after President Clinton raised taxes. And when, over the past six decades, has economic growth been the slowest? In the wake of President George W. Bush's major tax cuts. The point here is not that tax cuts hinder growth or that tax increases accelerate growth. Rather, it's that tax rates, by themselves, don't drive an economy.

What does? No single force. But one thing does have a very good track record: investment.

Investment, in economic terms, is money spent on new factories, office buildings, software, roads, scientific research, and anything else likely to yield future benefits. Most investment is—and should be—done by the private sector. But what's interesting, when you attempt to discern the causes of the American growth slowdown, is what has happened to private-sector investment relative to government investment. Private-sector investment, as measured by the Commerce Department, hasn't changed much over time. It was equal to 17 percent of GDP fifty years ago and it is about 17 percent now. But investment by the government— federal, state and local—has changed. It has dropped from about 7 percent of GDP in the 1950s to about 4 percent today.

Governments have a unique role to play in making investments for two main reasons. Some activities, like mass transportation and pollution reduction, have societal benefits but not necessarily financial ones, and the private sector simply won't undertake them. And while many other kinds of investments do bring big financial returns, only a fraction of those returns go to the original investor. This makes the private sector reluctant to jump in. As a result, economists say that the private sector tends to spend less on research and investment than is economically ideal.

Historically, the government has stepped into the void and helped create new industries with its investments. In the 1950s and 1960s, the G.I. Bill created a generation of college graduates, while the Interstate System of highways made the entire economy more productive. Later, the Defense Department developed the Internet, which spawned AOL, Google, and the rest. The late 1990s Internet boom was the only sustained period in the last thirty-five years when the economy grew at 4 percent a year. It was also the only time in the past thirty-five years when the incomes of the poor and the middle class rose at a healthy pace. Growth doesn't ensure rising living standards for everyone, but it sure helps.

Today, however, the United States is suffering from what I call investment-deficit disorder. You can find examples of this disorder in just about any realm of American life. Walk into a doctor's office and you will be asked to fill out a long form with the most basic kinds of information that you have provided dozens of times before. Walk into a doctor's office in many other rich countries and that information—as well as your medical history—will be stored digitally. These electronic records not only reduce hassle; they also reduce medical errors. The United States spends 16 percent of our economy on health care, compared with the 10 percent many rich countries spend, yet we cannot avail ourselves of electronic medical records. We are spending our money on medical treatments—many of which have only marginal health benefits—rather than investing it in ways that would have far broader benefits.

Along similar lines, Americans are indefatigable buyers of consumer electronics, yet a smaller share of households in the United States has broadband Internet service than in Canada, Japan, Britain, South Korea, and about a dozen other countries. Then there is transportation: A trip from Boston to Washington on the fastest train in this country takes six-and-a-half hours. A trip from Paris to Marseilles, roughly the same distance, takes three hours. And, above all, education: This country once led the world in educational attainment by a wide margin. It no longer does.

Education can often seem like one of the most discussed and yet one of the most confusing topics in the public debate. On the one hand, politicians offer platitudes about the importance of education in seemingly every campaign. On the other hand, you can come off as a purveyor of unconventional wisdom by asking whether education is overrated.

The television show *20/20* recently ran a segment asking whether college was worth it. The lyrics of pop songs, by everyone from the Indigo Girls to Kanye West, have raised their own version of such skepticism.[4] Liberals are especially likely to raise such doubts; the unemployment of college graduates is a favorite subject of research by the economists at the Economic Policy Institute, a labor-friendly think tank. Conservatives sometimes make their own version of a similar argument: Charles Murray, the co-author of *The Bell Curve*, recently wrote that trying to expand the ranks of college graduates was not worth it.

Fortunately, American society has conducted an enormous natural experiment over the last few decades on precisely the question of how much education matters.

In the experiment, one big group of Americans has become vastly more educated, while another group has not. In the process, they have allowed us to make some judgments about the role that education plays in spurring economic growth. For the sake of simplicity, we can refer to the first group—the one that became vastly more educated—as "women." The second group will be called "men."

From the founding of the country's first (all-male) colleges in the seventeenth century until just a few decades ago, men received far more education than women. But the two sexes have now switched places in a remarkably short period of time. For the last four decades, somewhere between 30 and 35 percent of men have graduated from a four-year college by the time they turned thirty-five. The shifts have been small. The story is quite different for women. In the 1960s, only 25 percent of women received a college degree; today, almost 40 percent of young women will end up with one. At most commencement ceremonies these days, women outnumber men.

And the returns that women have received on their added education have been enormous. Armed with college degrees, large numbers of women have entered fields once dominated by men. Nearly half of new doctors today are women, up from just one of every ten in the early 1970s. In all, the average inflation-adjusted weekly pay of women has jumped 26 percent since 1980. The average inflation-adjusted weekly pay of men has risen just 1 percent since 1980.

Education obviously isn't the only reason. Sexism has become less prevalent in recent decades, and today's female college graduates are less likely than their mothers and grandmothers to choose modest-paying jobs, like teaching. The decline of manufacturing jobs, meanwhile, has disproportionately hurt men. But research by Francine Blau and Lawrence Kahn of Cornell suggests that, over the past two decades, education played the biggest role in narrowing the pay gap.

The evidence for education's unique role in lifting economic growth is by no means limited to this natural experiment. The two most affluent immigrant groups in modern America—Asian Americans and Jews—are also the most highly educated. A rich body of economic literature has found that countries that educate more of their citizens tend to grow faster in subsequent years than similar countries that do not. The same is true of states and regions within this country. What distinguishes thriving Boston from the other struggling cities of New England? What distinguishes Minnesota from its poorer neighbors? Part of the answer is the relative share of native children who graduate from college.[5]

In their recent book, *The Race Between Education and Technology*, the economists Claudia Goldin and Lawrence Katz offer a historically rich argument for putting education at the top of any economic-growth strategy. One of their most subversive claims is that their fellow economists have exaggerated the importance of technological change. They argue that the ebb and flow in the supply of educated workers explains much of the changes in inequality over the past century. When one has risen, the other has generally fallen. When there have been more educated workers, they have been able to share the economy's bounty. When educational gains have slowed, as over the past few decades, the relatively scarce pool of educated workers has taken home a bigger potion of the nation's economy.

This, in turn, suggests that the demand for educated workers has been increasing at a fairly steady pace over the past century—and that demand can't be the main story. Yes, the Internet places a greater premium on education. But so did the personal computer and the mainframe. So did the jet engine, the automobile, and the telephone. Education, then, has been the most powerful driver of growth and of inequality.

Education is obviously not a magic potion. Anyone can name exceptions to the rule. Bill Gates didn't graduate from college (though, as Malcom Gladwell explained in his recent book, *Outliers*, Gates received an intense computer programming education while in high school). Some college graduates struggle to make a good living, and many will lose their jobs in this recession. But making policy based on these exceptions would be akin to getting rid of drunk-driving laws because some drunk drivers do not crash their cars.

Education, in the simplest terms, appears to be the best single bet that a society or an individual can make. It is the lifeblood of economic growth. At the most basic level, education helps people figure out how to make objects and accomplish tasks with less effort—which, in turn, allows them to make and do more. It helps a society leverage every other investment it makes, be it in alternative energy, science, or medicine.

Clearly, a growth agenda cannot be merely about education. It will also have to include other investments. And it will have to include a serious approach to the federal government's enormous looming budget deficits.

Taxes will almost certainly have to rise. They have averaged about 18 percent of gross domestic product for much of the past half-century, which is in some ways historically anomalous. Adolf Wagner, a nineteenth-century German economist, argued that taxes would tend to rise as societies became wealthier, and his prediction was borne out for much of the last two centuries. "As people grew more affluent," Matt Miller, a consultant for McKinsey & Company and a former Clinton administration official, wrote recently, "they'd want more of what only government could provide—a strong military, public order, good schools, and assorted welfare benefits, services that private citizens would have trouble arranging for on their own."[6] The idea is known as Wagner's Law.[7]

In recent decades, the United States has indeed spent more and more money on its military, on social benefits like Medicare, and on other government programs. But it hasn't raised the taxes necessary to pay for these programs. The government is now left with deficits that are truly frightening.

Even if taxes rise, though, that won't be enough. Spending will need to be reduced, too. In particular, the growth of health care spending—the single largest long-term threat to the budget—will need to be slowed.

As of mid-July 2009, it was too early to know what the fate of health reform would be. But the early months of negotiations suggested that failure was a possibility. Even if Congress passed a health care reform bill, it would not necessarily be one that slowed the growth of spending. The early versions of a bill produced by Congress expanded health insurance but did little to alter the flawed incentives inherent in this country's fee-for-service medical system.

These early negotiations on health care captured what is likely the single biggest threat to a serious economic-growth strategy: The current structure of the economy—the investment-deficit-disorder economy—benefits a lot of people. Many doctors, hospitals, and drug companies profit from a medical system that pays for care regardless of whether it brings better health. Teachers' unions benefit from an education system in which performance is rarely measured, let alone rewarded or punished. The producers of carbon-emitting energies benefit from an economy in which people do not have to bear the full societal cost of their pollution. Business executives and Wall Street traders have benefited from a lack of government oversight and a sharp fall in top marginal tax rates.

Each of these groups—and many others—can construct an argument for why their favorable treatment, in fact, benefits the rest of the American economy, too. Some of these arguments may even have merit. But the overall picture is a disturbing one. As a country, we have not managed to make hard economic choices or to put together a serious strategy for economic growth—the kind of strategy that has worked here in the past and is working today in other countries.

Paul Romer, the Stanford economist, compares economic growth to the Biblical notions of hope and charity. Hope, he says, is the promise that our children can live better than we do. Charity is our desire for other people's children to live better, as well. "These things are logically inconsistent without growth,"[8] as he says. Only growth makes it possible for one group of people to prosper without having to do so at the expense of another.

Of course, economic growth—wealth—is also a crucial source of global power. And there is nothing inevitable about the United States remaining the wealthiest country in the world.

David Leonhardt is an economics columnist at the *New York Times*. He is concurrently a staff writer for the *New York Times Magazine* and a contributor to the *Times*' Economix blog. Mr. Leonhardt joined the *Times* in 1999. In 2004, he founded Keeping Score, an analytical sports column in the Sunday *Times*. Previously, Mr. Leonhardt worked for *Business Week* magazine, in Chicago and New York, and for the metro desk of the *Washington Post*. He earned a B.S. in applied mathematics from Yale University.

[1] Carmen M. Reinhart and Kenneth S. Rogoff, "The Aftermath of Financial Crises" (paper prepared for presentation at the American Economic Association meetings, San Francisco, CA, 3 January 2009).

[2] Lawrence H. Summers, "Responding to an Historic Economic Crisis: The Obama Program" (speech, Brookings Institution, Washington, D.C., 13 March 2009). The speech is available at http://www.brookings.edu/~/media/Files/events/2009/0313_summers/20090313_summers.pdf

[3] Paul M. Romer, "Economic Growth," in *The Concise Encyclopedia of Economics*, ed. David R. Henderson (Indianapolis: Liberty Fund, 2007).

[4] In "Closer to Fine" the Indigo Girls sing about having "spent four years prostrate to the higher mind, got my paper and I was free." In Kanye West's debut album, *College Dropout*, he gives his take on the career ladder for college graduates at the Gap: entry-level position, followed by kissing up to the boss, followed by a promotion to the secretary's secretary.

[5] For local policymakers who worry that they will lose the students they educate to more prosperous cities elsewhere, this sentence is worth a close rereading. Educating native children tends to lift growth. "Brain drain" is not as big a problem as is often assumed.

[6] Matt Miller, *The Tyranny of Dead Ideas* (New York: Times Books, 2009).

[7] At Economix, a *New York Times* blog, we have started something called Club Wagner. To join, you simply acknowledge that taxes need to rise. A list of the bipartisan membership is available at http://economix.blogs.nytimes.com/2009/07/09/more-members-of-club-wagner/ or by typing "Club Wagner" into Google.

[8] Paul Romer, "Risk and Return" (commencement address, Albertson College, 1 June 1996).

Part **2**

"The most important effects of the financial crisis and subsequent recession may be the least tangible: a serious worldwide erosion of confidence in American competence and in willingness to follow U.S. initiatives."

— RICHARD N. COOPER

Global Recession and National Security

Richard N. Cooper
Maurits C. Boas Professor of International Economics
Harvard University

The world is in the worst recession since before World War II. World trade will decline for the first time since 1982. China, Egypt, India, and Indonesia will still show positive growth in 2009, although much below the preceding years; they are among the few. Most countries, including all the rich countries, will experience economic declines (as measured by real GDP) in 2009, and most are expected to have only modest growth in 2010 (see Table 1). The extreme risk aversion in the financial sector that was seen during the fall of 2008 has not been experienced since 1931—not a good year—nearly eight decades ago. There has been some return toward normalcy since then, but it has been halting and tentative. Exceptional uncertainty about the timing and pace of recovery remain.

It is worth noting that the years 2002 to 2007 were exceptionally good years for the world economy, perhaps the best such period in history. Growth was robust and widespread, inflation was low, and prices of primary products firmed. Against this background, many people around the world, especially young people, formed expectations about the future that were dashed in 2008-2009, resulting in puzzlement, disillusionment, and anger.

Here is not the place to review the causes of the downturn, except to note that it began unambiguously in the United States with an over-exuberant residential construction fueled by easy access to mortgages, especially by parts of the population that had not previously qualified for residential mortgages, resulting in the so-called subprime mortgage crisis. It is a reflection of the globalization of financial markets that this quintessentially local form of finance created problems in financial institutions around the world, starting in February 2007 with HSBC, but spreading especially to Europe, where a number of financial institutions held securitized U.S. mortgages (in the form of mortgage-backed securities and collateralized debt obligations) and others were dependent on short-term borrowing which became unavailable once the mortgage problem surfaced seriously. Moreover, the subsequent U.S. recession, starting with the collapse of housing construction, quickly spread to the rest of the world through a rise in U.S. household savings rates and a decline in U.S. imports. So much for decoupling. It should be added that while the recession began in the United States and the initial decline in aggregate demand was most serious here, other sources of declining demand could be found in China, Britain, and Spain, where housing construction had also become too exuberant to last.

This paper will address the tangible and intangible consequences of the worldwide recession and their implications for U.S. national security.

The tangible consequences involve the decline in trade, private capital flows, remittances, and possibly foreign assistance to many countries in the world caused by the worldwide recession. These declines, in turn, will lead to slower growth or even declines in production and income, returning foreign workers, and higher unemployment around the world.

The decline in world trade in 2008-2009 contrasts with the annual growth in trade volume in excess of 7 percent just a few years ago. Trade-related jobs—a major source of income in the developing world, drawing workers from the countryside to urban centers—will disappear, contributing to millions of lay-offs and few prospects for migrant workers. For example, it is said that in China over twenty million internal migrants have lost their jobs, mainly in low-skilled manufacturing and construction. In addition, several million newly graduated university students will have difficulty finding jobs in the current economic environment. The Chinese authorities are greatly concerned about the eruption of social unrest and have already acted to head it off, namely by providing self-employment loans to new graduates and by taking steps to increase real living standards in rural areas. Both initiatives are part of a much larger fiscal stimulus package, which also emphasizes construction of new infrastructure such as railroads, highways, ports, clinics, and schools.

In the oil-exporting Arab Gulf countries, the decline in new jobs will mainly impact foreigners rather than residents, since most of the work in the private sector, and much in the public sector, is performed by temporary migrants. Budget cuts may also reduce the incomes of citizens, although these countries typically have substantial public savings on which they could draw to avoid any major reduction.

Private capital inflows to developing countries exceeded $550 billion in 2007, and remittances from workers abroad are estimated to have exceeded $300 billion, both far in excess of official foreign assistance, which remained below $90 billion. On one estimate, remittances will decline by 10 percent in 2009 and private capital flows will fall by far more than that, leaving countries such as Pakistan and the Philippines short of foreign exchange, funds for investment, and income for families of workers abroad. The United States, Saudi Arabia, and Switzerland are estimated to be the three largest sources of remittances, but other European and Arab Gulf countries are not far behind. During the first quarter of 2009, the Mexican government estimated that more Mexicans returned home than left for the United States, the first reversal on record.

The recruiting ground for terrorists, and for criminal gangs, is among idle, disaffected, and alienated young men; not typically the poorest people in the world, but those that by world standards would be considered "lower middle class." The recession will likely increase the numbers of such people, though perhaps not massively unless the recession becomes much worse than is now generally expected, or unless it produces serious protectionist, even xenophobic, reactions that prolong the decline of trade and prevent the hiring of foreigners.

Some countries are more vulnerable than others. Large numbers of Pakistanis working in the Persian Gulf region may lose their jobs. Pakistan already runs a current account deficit that will need to be financed as exports and remittances decline or be reduced by contracting imports, which usually means contracting production and employment. Many Yemenis work in Saudi Arabia and other Gulf countries. Mexico is experiencing a return of emigrants who have lost their jobs in the United States and cannot find new ones. As a result, Mexico will lose those remittances and returning workers will aggravate the growing problem of unemployment in Mexico, where exports and manufacturing production—especially in the automotive sector— have declined sharply. If inflows of private foreign capital decline, as they surely will, Mexico will have to reduce its substantial current account deficit in the absence of official support from traditional sources such as the International Monetary Fund and the United States. Colombia, South Africa, and Turkey also have significant current account deficits, as do several countries in central Europe. In the face of declines in private capital flows, these countries will require official support, contractions in imports and production, or both.

Rich countries typically have a social safety net that will limit the hardship created by higher unemployment. But their budget deficits will increase as a result of both declining revenues and increased social expenditures, automatic or deliberate. With higher budget deficits comes higher public debt, from levels that in many cases were already high (relative to GDP) before the recession (see Table 1 for budget deficits and current account deficits). Thus, there will be increased pressures on expenditures that are not seen as high priority, which for some U.S. allies will include defense expenditures. European governments, in particular, will meet greater public resistance under the circumstances to increases in defense expenditures, or even to maintaining current levels, and new NATO members will find it more difficult to meet their NATO commitments. (The exceptionally high budget deficits for the United States and Britain shown in Table 1 reflect large assistance to financial firms, much of which may be recouped as they return to normalcy and can repay the government support funds.)

Japan and South Korea, in contrast, may increase the priority of some defense expenditures despite the recession, thanks to the continual saber-rattling of North Korea. Japan and South Korea were both hard hit by a drop in exports in late 2008. The decline in exports discouraged investment. Unlike the Asian financial and economic crisis of 1997-1998, of which painful memories are still fresh, South Korea ran a modest current account surplus in early 2009 as imports fell more rapidly than exports, aided by a decline in prices of oil and other primary products. Also, South Korea had large reserves, over $200 billion. However, Korean banks (as in 1997) had extensive short-term foreign debt. The South Korean government chose not to rely on its reserves to cushion the fall in exports and the withdrawal of foreign capital from South Korea's stock market, and instead allowed its currency to depreciate substantially, from near 900 to over 1,500 won to the dollar, before rebounding to 1,275 in early June. Since the Japanese yen appreciated against the dollar, the won/yen rate greatly increased the competitiveness of Korean goods, thus cushioning the fall of South Korea's exports, albeit at the expense of Japan, whose exports fell 47 percent, as against 25 percent for South Korea.

The South Korean authorities sharply lowered interest rates in late 2008 and took other steps to ease credit, on which Korean business depends heavily. Special programs were introduced for small and medium enterprises, which account for most urban employment and are especially vulnerable to a credit crunch. Government expenditure rose sharply in early 2009, despite a decline in revenue, thus leading to an expected 2009 budget deficit of 5.6 percent of GDP.

Japan had an exceptionally large drop in GDP in late 2008, contracting at an annual pace of 12 percent from October through December, the sharpest since the oil shock of 1974. In April, following the G-20 meeting, Japan announced a new stimulus package of fifteen trillion yen, around 3 percent of GDP. But

Japan's public debt is already large and a serious pessimism pervades the Japanese business community, with many Japanese fearing another "lost decade." It will be difficult in these circumstances for Japan to follow through with its stated intention of helping finance the movement of U.S. marines from Okinawa to Guam.

The recession carries a few pluses with respect to U.S. security and general well-being in the world. One of the characteristics of the 2002 to 2007 global boom was a sharp rise in the prices of primary products, especially petroleum—which is used for cooking in many poor countries in the form of kerosene and for transport—and staple foods such as rice, wheat, corn, and vegetable oils. This created great anxiety in many countries in 2008 about major social unrest, often leading to large government subsidies, especially for imported food. While they remain significantly higher than they were six years ago, prices for these products have fallen substantially since mid-2008. Social and budgetary pressures on this account have greatly eased. Of course, producers of foodstuffs—assuming the rise in world prices was passed on to farmers, which was not always the case—will have lower incomes. But the potential social problems were mainly in urban areas, where consumers predominate. The World Bank estimates that more than half of developing countries will benefit from the declines in food prices.[1]

The oil revenues of all oil-exporting countries, while higher than earlier in the decade, have declined sharply from the elevated levels of late 2007 and the first half of 2008, when oil prices briefly exceeded $140 a barrel. This includes, of course, the revenues of Iraq, complicating the normalization of that country and perhaps prolonging the need for U.S. financial support. But it also includes the revenues of Iran, Russia, and Venezuela, each of which in different ways has challenged the policies of the United States, greatly facilitated by high government and foreign exchange revenues. All three countries have become fiscally undisciplined and will have to cut their expenditures sharply in view of the decline in oil revenue, unless they are willing to countenance a sharp increase in already double-digit levels of domestic inflation, which would increase domestic disaffection with their respective governments. The decline in oil prices is directly linked to the slowdown in world economic activity, so in this respect the slowdown can be said to benefit U.S. national security. Concretely, Iran will have to balance more carefully its financial and material support to Hezbollah and the pace of its nuclear and missile programs against pressing requirements for domestic expenditure.

Oil and gas accounted for over 60 percent of Russian exports in 2007 and half of the government's revenue. Exports of oil and gas rose from around $50 billion in 2000 to $200 billion in 2007, with both price increases and increased production contributing to the rise. In 2008 prices rose further, but production fell somewhat. In 2009 Russia's current account surplus moved into deficit, and the budget deficit is expected to exceed 8 percent of GDP. Sales of oil and gas delivered ever rising prosperity to the Russian people during the 2000s, as well as respect, and even admiration, for the Putin government. Russians, like people everywhere, often confuse coincidence with causation. The Putin government, in turn, used growing government revenue to pursue a more aggressive foreign and defense policy, especially toward Russia's "near abroad" (the former Soviet republics), including Estonia and Ukraine and actually invaded Georgia in August 2008, subsequently recognizing Abkhazia and South Ossetia as independent states. Russia also used its increased revenue to pay down its public external debt (much of it inherited from the Soviet Union), although private Russian corporations relied heavily on Western capital to engage in production and acquisitions, having accumulated nearly half a trillion dollars in debt by late 2008. Russia built up foreign exchange reserves to $600 billion by mid-2008, but these dropped $210 billion by March 2009, as Russia defended its currency against declining oil revenues and non-rollover of foreign loans to Russian firms. Even so, the ruble depreciated from twenty-four to the dollar in May 2008 to thirty-one to the dollar in May 2009. No serious economic reforms were undertaken since the aftermath of the 1998 financial crisis, and by the end of the decade the Russian economy was in bad shape, including agriculture, old manufacturing, and oil exploration. Oil production was in decline as older fields were depleted and not replaced with new development. The Russian government used its revenue to support old manufacturing (such as production of the Lada) and to acquire shares in firms that had earlier been privatized.

Anders Aslund and Andrew Kuchins aver that Russian foreign policy has become more pro-Western in periods of low oil prices and less pro-Western in periods of high oil prices.[2] This remains to be seen during the 2009 downturn in prices—along with how long the lower prices last. Russia explicitly backed away from pressing ahead with World Trade Organization membership after the invasion of Georgia in August 2008 (as WTO members, both Georgia and Ukraine could blackball Russia's new membership), but indicated once again in June 2009 that it would like to join the WTO by completing the accession negotiations. Moscow also announced that it would like to join the Paris-based Organization for Economic Cooperation and Development, a so-called rich-country discussion organization, but one that would entail commitment to (or explicit derogation from) the many codes of behavior that have been negotiated in the OECD over the years.

This is not the place to review the budgetary priorities of the United States or the congressional and presidential decisions that determine them. It is widely agreed that U.S. national security could be enhanced by raising non-defense spending under the heading of international affairs (including more political reporting by diplomats, more public diplomacy, and more foreign aid)—if necessary, by reducing defense spending. In a recession, congressional resistance to cutting defense procurement is likely to be severe, so a security-enhancing reallocation of funds is less likely to occur.

The most important effects of the financial crisis and subsequent recession may be the least tangible: a serious worldwide erosion of confidence in American competence and in willingness to follow U.S. initiatives. High respect for American competence, even by those who disliked the U.S. government or shunned so-called U.S. values, almost carried a sense of invincibility. The rest of the world typically placed more confidence in American competence than was warranted—most Americans knew better. But the events of the past eight years, starting with the successful hijacking of four airplanes used for an attack on the Pentagon and the World Trade Center, have put American competence in severe doubt. One terrible event could plausibly be attributed to bad luck or to having let one's guard down temporarily. But 9/11 was followed by the post-combat phase in Iraq, which the United States is generally considered to have bungled. This was reinforced by a perceived debacle in handling Hurricane Katrina. Now the subprime mortgage crisis, at the heart of the seemingly efficient and invincible American financial system, leading to a wider financial crisis followed by a U.S. and global recession, further undermines confidence in American competence. The crisis clearly started in the United States, not in some emerging market, or, as in 1992, in Europe. How was it allowed to happen? Who was asleep at the switch, and why? These events have produced a loss of respect around the world for the United States and for American-style capitalism. Chinese reformers complain that they have lost their "template." French and Chinese "models" are in ascendance. There will be less inclination to follow U.S. leadership, and there is even widespread talk of negative implications for the international role of the U.S. dollar, although, in reality, alternatives will not be easy to find.[3]

The loss of a sense of U.S. invincibility may embolden existing hostile groups to attempt—through some dramatic act—to bring the system of American capitalism, now apparently vulnerable, crashing down for good; the optimum time to attempt that has, perhaps, happily now passed.

President Obama will have opportunities to reestablish America's reputation for competence. He commands tremendous good will around the world, and has nurtured it well during his first year in office. But to reestablish a reputation for competence will require a series of effective actions, not just agreeable speech.

Table 1

	Projected Growth in GDP		Deficits	
	2009	2010	Government	Current Account[a]
	(percent)		2009, percent of GDP	
USA	-2.8	1.6	13.2	3.2
Canada	-2.3	1.7	2.3	1.9
Japan	-6.7	0.8	6.3	-1.7
Korea, South	-6.0	0.4	5.6	-1.2
Britain	-3.7	0.6	13.8	1.6
Euroland	-4.1	0.5	5.7	1.0
Germany	-5.5	0.5	4.4	-4.4
France	-2.8	0.5	6.6	2.2
Italy	-4.4	0.3	5.3	2.6
Spain	-3.5	-0.5	9.6	7.5
Poland	-0.8	1.5	3.8	5.2
Turkey	-4.5	1.0	5.3	1.3
Russia	-5.0	2.0	8.4	0.6
China	6.5	7.3	3.5	-6.9
India	5.0	6.4	7.7	3.0
Indonesia	2.4	3.2	3.2	-0.5
Pakistan	-0.9	2.0	5.6	1.2
Thailand	-4.4	1.1	4.7	-2.7
Brazil	-1.5	2.7	2.0	1.2
Colombia	-2.0	1.8	3.4	3.9
Mexico	-4.4	1.2	5.3	3.1
Venezuela	-5.0	-5.4	5.3	-0.4
Saudi Arabia	-1.0	3.3	5.8	8.4
Egypt	3.4	3.1	7.0	0.8
South Africa	-1.8	3.1	4.0	5.6

* a minus sign signifies a surplus

* Source: *The Economist*, 6 June 2009

Richard Cooper is the Maurits C. Boas Professor of International Economics at Harvard University. Dr. Cooper also served as chairman of the National Intelligence Council, from 1995 to 1997; chairman of Federal Reserve Bank of Boston, from 1990 to 1992, Under-Secretary of State for Economic Affairs, from 1977 to 1981; and Deputy Assistant Secretary of State for International Monetary Affairs, from 1965 to 1966. Previously, Dr. Cooper was the Frank Altschul Professor of International Economics, from 1966 to 1977, and Provost, from 1972 to 1974 at Yale University and senior staff economist at the Council of Economic Advisers, from 1961 to 1963. Dr. Cooper is on the board of trustees for the Center for Naval Analyses. Dr. Cooper was a Marshall Scholar and a recipient of the National Intelligence Distinguished Service Medal. He received an A.B. from Oberlin College, a M.Sc. from the London School of Economics and Political Science, and a Ph.D. from Harvard.

[1] "Global Economic Prospects 2009," The World Bank, 22 June 2009, 45.

[2] Anders Aslund and Andrew Kuchins, *The Russia Balance Sheet* (Washington: Peterson Institute for International Economics, 2009).

[3] See Richard N. Cooper, "The Future of the Dollar," Policy Brief 09-21 (Washington: Peterson Institute for International Economics, September 2009).

"The current obsession with not repeating the mistakes of the past suggests that the United States is learning the wrong trade lesson from the global economic crisis and that Washington risks gearing up to fight a war against incipient protectionism, rather than devising a strategy to avoid repeating the mistakes that led to the current economic crisis."

— BRUCE STOKES

Rebalancing Economic Engagement:
The Foreign Policy Consequences

Bruce Stokes
International Economics Columnist
National Journal

Hard times and protectionism have long gone hand-in-hand. The Great Depression and Smoot-Hawley are forever linked in the public imagination. Without a doubt, vigilance is called for lest the Great Recession lead nations to turn inward once again.

But the widely-accepted narrative that the global economy is in some proto-protectionist period does not comport with current experience or with new public opinion data. "Resort to high intensity protectionist measures has been contained overall, albeit with difficulties," concluded a World Trade Organization report in July 2009.[1] And recent polling data show support for trade strengthening, not weakening, even in the United States.

The current obsession with not repeating the mistakes of the past suggests that the United States is learning the wrong trade lesson from the global economic crisis and that Washington risks gearing up to fight a war against incipient protectionism, rather than devising a strategy to avoid repeating the mistakes that led to the current economic crisis.

The financial meltdown that spawned the Great Recession was rooted in the global current account imbalances that emerged over the last decade. These imbalances were, in part, a product of exchange rate, monetary, banking, and trade policies. Reestablishing more sustainable balances will require a new global economic growth strategy, in which trade policy will play a minor, but important, role.

In the process of rebalancing, the United States will produce more of what it consumes, while China, Germany, and Japan, among others, will consume more of what they produce. To facilitate this transition, Washington is likely to put new emphasis on reciprocity and a balance of benefits in trade relationships. The dollar is likely to weaken. A more aggressive U.S. trade posture is likely to worsen trade relations with a number of countries, particularly China. And, with multilateral and bilateral trade negotiations stalemated, Washington's approach to trade liberalization may become more results oriented.

As American trade policy evolves from one shaped by the Great Depression to one reflecting the lessons of the Great Recession, foreign policy consequences are unavoidable. U.S. international leadership built on Americans living beyond their means is unsustainable. Actions Washington is likely to take to gain some control over its international accounts will undoubtedly anger many allies. And recent congressional opposition to the South Korea free trade agreement is a sign that strategic and diplomatic interests can no longer be counted on to trump trade interests.

But, in the long run, an American economy that is more stable and less dependent on debt, both domestic and foreign, will be stronger and provide the basis for a more robust U.S. foreign policy.

The Historical Pattern

The Great Recession put the American economy in unchartered territory. The sharp contraction in economic growth rivaled that of the Great Depression. The collapse in industrial production exceeded that of recent downturns. The downturn in the labor market was the worst in the modern era. And trade declined more rapidly than at any time since the 1930s.

In the past, crises of this magnitude have sparked trade policy reactions in the United States and around the world. As the depression tightened its grip on the American economy in 1930, farmers and industrialists clamored for protection from foreign competition. Congress responded by passing what came to be known as the Smoot-Hawley Tariff Act, raising duties on 890 items. Smoot-Hawley did not cause the depression, but it certainly helped deepen it. Douglas Irwin, an economist at Dartmouth University, estimates that Smoot-Hawley reduced total U.S. imports by 4 to 6 percent.[2] Other nations also raised their tariffs, contributing to a two-thirds decline in world trade between 1929 and 1933.

The economic troubles of the early 1980s evoked a similar protectionist response by the United States. Reacting to the double-dip recession at the beginning of the decade, double-digit unemployment, and an unprecedented trade deficit, the Reagan administration, often in an effort to head-off even more restrictive congressional action, imposed the most protectionist measures seen since Herbert Hoover. Curbs were placed on imports of a range of items, including autos, steel, semi-conductors, and machine tools. At the time, economist David Hale calculated that about 8 percent of all U.S. imports became subject to some kind of restraint. (Less than 1 percent of U.S. imports are controlled today.)

The Current Crisis

In the run-up to the 2008 financial crisis and Great Recession, the growth in global commerce consistently outpaced the expansion of the world economy. Trade fueled growth. Now the lack of this fuel inhibits the restarting of the global growth engine.

Monthly exports and imports by major developed and developing economies began falling in September 2008 and global commerce grew by only 1.5 percent for the year. The World Bank predicted that global trade in goods and services might drop by as much as 6.1 percent in 2009, the largest such decline in eighty years. The United States has been particularly hard hit. American exports and imports of goods and services were down 24.9 percent in the first quarter of 2009 compared with the same quarter in 2008.

As in past periods of global economic contraction, nations moved to protect their domestic producers. The number of anti-dumping cases jumped 27.6 percent worldwide in 2008 over 2007. Brazil imposed 12 to 14 percent duties on certain steel products after exempting them from tariffs since 2005. India placed a tariff on soybean oil. The European Community reintroduced export subsidies for milk and butter. All together, the World Trade Organization (WTO) classified as restrictive eighty-three trade measures taken by twenty-four nations and the European Union.

Many of these actions were what economists Simon Evenett and Richard Baldwin termed "murky protectionism."[3] Nations reintroduced tariffs or practices they had voluntarily curbed and thus did not violate their WTO obligations. Or governments merely continued activities they never agreed to forego in the first place. China, for example, which promised to spend $173 billion to stimulate its economy, banned all local, provincial, and national public agencies from buying most imported goods with that money. Since China is not a signatory to the WTO public procurement code, Beijing was violating no international obligation.

The Buy American provisions of the American Recovery and Reinvestment Act—the stimulus package—highlighted the insidious nature of "murky protectionism." The Obama administration promised to live up to its international commitments with regard to public procurement funded by this legislation. But American states do much of this spending, and thirteen of them, including Ohio, New Jersey, and Virginia, are not party to the WTO public procurement code. Moreover, the devil is always in the detail of spending legislation. In April, the Environmental Protection Agency issued guidance that all iron, steel, and manufactured goods used in $6 billion worth of spending to improve drinking water must be American-made unless a waiver is granted.

In addition, nations provided massive subsidies to banks, automakers, and others with the blatant intention of altering the competitive landscape. France created a $7.6 billion fund to invest in French companies so that France can "continue to be a country where we build cars, boats, trains and planes," in the words of French president Nicolas Sarkozy.[4] And a prerequisite of Berlin's help for Opel was a commitment from that beleaguered automaker to close plants in Belgium, rather than Germany.

But this proved more smoke than fire. "To date we have not observed large scale increases in the level of discrimination against foreign suppliers of goods and services by major trading states," concluded a mid-2009 study by the World Bank and the Center for Economic Policy Research in London.[5]

The Public Mood

Nevertheless, the growing proclivity toward nationalist trade policies reflected overwhelming and widespread sentiment that governments should take whatever steps necessary to protect their economies, even if friendly governments objected to those measures.

Public support for trade, at least in the United States, has declined this decade. In 2009, 65 percent of Americans said trade was good for the nation, according to a recent survey by the Pew Global Attitudes Project. That figure was down from 78 percent in 2002. And support for trade was lower in the United States than in all but one of the twenty-five countries Pew surveyed.[6]

More ominously, Americans have lost faith in the benefits of trade. Pew surveys show that a majority of those questioned believe that trade kills more jobs than it creates and that it lowers wages. And a plurality believes trade leads to higher, not lower, prices.

Such attitudes are evident in the evolving composition of the Democratic caucus in the U.S. House of Representatives. More than four dozen new Democrats have joined the House over the last two elections, and a significant proportion of them are critics of trade. Their opposition to the Colombia, Panama, and South Korea free trade agreements has blocked their passage, and they are likely to continue to impede a vote, possibly until spring 2010 or even 2011, if then. The killing of union leaders in Colombia went up in 2008, not down, hardly a sign of progress on an issue Democrats say is key. And opening the door for Hyundai to increase its share of the U.S. market at a time when the American taxpayer is bailing out Detroit is a political non-starter. The auto portion of the South Korea deal will have to be renegotiated to improve U.S. access to the Korean market.

But the oft-repeated narrative that bad times have sparked a populist, protectionist reaction is not supported by the most recent public opinion data, which is far more nuanced. Americans' reaction to the economic crisis has been to see global markets as an opportunity, not a threat. In April 2009, 56 percent of the U.S. public said that trade could boost economic growth, up from 46 percent who thought that way in October 2007, according to a CNN poll.[7]

Polling data also suggest that the American public is schizophrenic about trade. Americans continue to support open markets and are generally suspicious of big government subsidies for specific industries. Just 36 percent back the bailout of Detroit. But they also think government policies should benefit Americans, not foreigners. They remain wary of free trade agreements. And they support specific restrictive actions for specific purposes, such as raising trade barriers to protect steelworker jobs.

As economic conditions worsen, especially unemployment, pressure for a protectionist response is likely to grow. There will undoubtedly be an uptick in defensive trade actions. The auto bailout and the widespread support for creating green jobs are signs that industrial policy has new life.

Thus, the need for wariness about protectionism remains strong. But immediate trade policy issues—such as the Buy American controversy and bailouts—should not divert attention from the lessons of the economic crisis and recent failed efforts at trade liberalization that will ultimately shape future U.S. trade policy.

The Lessons

About a decade ago, substantial current account imbalances began to emerge in the world economy. In 2001, the U.S. current account deficit was 3.8 percent of GDP. By 2007 it had nearly doubled to 5.2 percent. China, meanwhile, ran a current account surplus equal to 11.4 percent of GDP in 2007, Germany a surplus of 7.6 percent, and Japan a surplus of 4.8 percent.

These imbalances reflected different patterns of national savings and investment that were a product of inflexible exchange rates, differences in monetary policy and financial regulation, and, to a modest extent, trade policy.

To balance national ledgers, these imbalances required ever-more innovative recycling of funds that ultimately proved unsafe, and the global financial crisis ensued. Avoiding similar problems in the future requires the prevention of the reemergence of destabilizing current account imbalances.

Most economists believe the United States can safely maintain a current account deficit of about 2 to 3 percent of GDP. The U.S. current account deficit has declined, thanks to the recession, a dramatic rise in private saving, and a fall off in the trade imbalance. But if, as many economists expect, the United States is the first nation to recover from the global downturn, its current account is poised to worsen again. "If we return to external deficits that led to this crisis," warned European Central Bank president Jean-Claude Trichet recently, "we'll have the recipe for a new crisis."[8]

To avoid that eventuality requires domestic reform. The United States needs to save more and spend less, largely through policies to encourage private savings and curb government dissaving. The international consequence of this will be that Americans will produce more of what they consume, leaving the Chinese, Germans, and Japanese to consume more of what they produce.

Much of this could be achieved through a global currency realignment that involves a weakening of the dollar and a strengthening of the renminbi, the yen, and the euro, to make imports into the United States more expensive and American exports relatively less expensive.

This exchange rate realignment has long been resisted, especially by Beijing, Tokyo, and Berlin, who see it as Washington's "beggar-thy-neighbor" manipulation of currency values in lieu of improving the underlying competitiveness of American industry. Successive U.S. administrations have also supported a strong dollar as a means of containing domestic inflation, reassuring foreign holders of dollar-denominated assets, and as a symbol of and practical tool for the exercise of U.S. foreign policy.

Trade policy is no substitute for domestic reforms or currency realignment, but it can complement such efforts by fostering trade expansion at a time of threatening protectionism.   Unfortunately, the trade liberalizing paradigm that served the United States and the world so well for so long may have run its course.

The Uruguay Round of multilateral trade negotiations took seven years to complete. The current Doha Round is in its eighth year, with no prospect of a timely conclusion. Such protracted negotiations are of decreasing relevance to a business community operating on eighteen month product cycles.

The Obama administration claims it is committed to finishing the Doha Round. But U.S. manufacturers and service providers say what is on the table in Geneva is insufficient. The European Union seems ready to settle on the current text. A stronger government in India creates at least an opportunity for Delhi to show more leadership. And China has more to gain than most from a successful conclusion. The 1990-1991 recession helped convince governments engaged in the Uruguay Round to finally reach agreement. This may happen again with the Doha Round. But a significant portion of the American trade policy community thinks the round is dead. And just any deal will not necessarily be an economic triumph; Many of the most important obstacles to global commerce today are non-tariff trade barriers—primarily domestic regulatory practices affecting service industries—that are not part of the multilateral negotiation.

Bilateral and regional trade liberalization efforts may have similarly hit a wall. Exports to U.S. free trade partners have grown impressively in recent years. But the business community complains that most recent bilateral free trade agreements involve economies too small to merit the effort. And the Bush administration's strategy of signing free trade deals with Central America, Morocco, and others as a means of leveraging progress in the Doha Round failed. Moreover, there is little prospect of Congress approving the pending agreements with Panama, Colombia, and South Korea in 2009.

The pressing need to achieve more sustainable global current account balances and the disappointing track record of recent multilateral and bilateral trade negotiations suggest the need for a reframing of U.S. trade policy.

The United States has long championed the principle of most-favored-nation (MFN) treatment in the General Agreement on Tariffs and Trade and its successor, the World Trade Organization. To avoid discrimination, MFN requires that any concession granted one nation must be accorded to all.

But MFN creates a free-rider problem. In the Doha Round, MFN has inhibited efforts to reach sector-specific agreements eliminating all tariffs on products such as chemicals, paper, and environmentally-significant technologies. Major producers have been reluctant to strike such deals because they would then have to extend the benefits to all producers, even if those nations did not open their markets.

When tariffs were uniformly high, MFN helped prevent trade distortion. Now that tariffs are relatively low, the economic wisdom of letting foot draggers hold back nations that want to completely eliminate duties that are effectively nuisance taxes is open to question. Multi-speed trade liberalization, in which like-minded nations—a coalition of the willing—achieve benefits commensurate with the concessions they are willing to make, while others move more slowly, has growing support among many trade experts and business leaders.

At the same time, there may need to be a renewed emphasis on reciprocity and a balance of benefits in international trade agreements.

"The starting assumption has been that the obligations undertaken by each country involve a balance of benefits," wrote the late Robert Hudec, an authority on international trade law, in *Development, Trade, and the WTO*, adding, "The benefits granted to others in the form of a country's own obligations, balanced against the benefits that country obtains from the obligations undertaken by others."[9]

Pursuit of a narrow balance in trade would be neither workable nor economically sound. But public support for trade has eroded precisely because people do not believe that trade agreements are fair or deliver sufficient value to the United States.

Reciprocity, with its implicit focus on promoting a country's exports rather than valuing imports, has long been derided as mercantilism. Economists argue that unilateral import liberalization benefits consumers and thus should be pursued even if it is nonreciprocal and a nation's exports do not increase. But this economic reasoning fails to address the unintended economic consequences when non-reciprocity contributes to unsustainable current account imbalances.

"Because of U.S. fealty to the free-trade ideology and geopolitical interest in having other countries support it," wrote Harvard University's Robert Lawrence and the Brookings Institution's Charles Schultz in 1990 in *An American Trade Strategy*, "the United States has in practice stopped negotiating for serious reciprocity."[10] That may have to change.

A trade policy in pursuit of reciprocity and a balance of benefits would necessarily redirect American trade strategy toward trade liberalization in sectors where the United States is most likely to benefit, such as services, and free trade agreements with major economies.

For example, the notion of a free trade agreement with Europe has been around for two decades. But it has repeatedly been rejected out of fear it would imperil multilateral negotiations. Those deliberations are either dead or will soon be completed. And the benefits of a single transatlantic market are demonstrable. The elimination of tariff and non-tariff barriers to transatlantic business would lift Americans' per capita income by up to 2.5 percent and Europeans' income by up to 3 percent, according to a 2005 study by the Organization for Economic Cooperation and Development.[11] And the U.S. Chamber of Commerce and Business Europe estimate that achievement of even a more limited agenda would add more than $10 billion to the transatlantic economy.[12] Moreover, if such a deal contained an open docking provision that allowed other nations to join if they similarly liberalized their markets, the benefits would spread.

The U.S. National Association of Manufacturers and Business Europe have studied the advantages and disadvantages of such an accord, and it is widely supported by a range of former U.S. trade officials. Alternatively, Washington and Brussels might consider a mutual elimination of all tariffs on manufactured products, as suggested by the Confederation of Danish and Swedish Industries, or the creation of a free trade area in services that the U.S. Coalition of Services Industries supports.

A $27 trillion U.S.-EU market with 800 million consumers that could establish common standards for a new cell phone or a clean automobile engine, for example, would create scale economies that would give European and American firms an advantage when competing with Chinese firms.

The disappointing track record of transatlantic regulatory harmonization efforts since 1995 and the problems encountered in negotiating the Australian free trade agreement underscore the difficulty of such a course. But the potential benefits are considerable, when measured against the current stalemate in trade liberalization. And such agreements could potentially change the domestic political dynamic around trade in the United States.

The Elephant in the Room

Any reframing of U.S. trade policy will necessarily affect trade relations with China. In 2008, a third of the U.S. merchandise trade deficit with the world was with the People's Republic. Economic theory teaches that bilateral trade imbalances do not matter. But if reducing the overall U.S. imbalance with the world is necessary, doing so without China bearing its fair share of the burden is a prescription for friction with others who do bear that load. In 2008, Japan accounted for 9.1 percent of the overall U.S. merchandise trade deficit and in the first quarter of 2009 it absorbed 9.3 percent of the rebalancing of the U.S. trade account. China, by comparison, absorbed only 5 percent of that U.S. rebalancing. Any reframing of U.S. trade policy in the wake of the recent economic crisis may require greater burden-sharing by China.

The Obama administration has backed off campaign pledges to press for further appreciation of the renminbi and has declined to cite Beijing for currency manipulation, in part out of recognition that China is America's largest creditor. And there is no meaningful pressure in Congress to force Beijing to appreciate.

But the rise in the productivity of China's economy has not been mirrored by a rise in the external purchasing power of its currency, and the real effective exchange rate of the renminbi remains undervalued, by somewhere between 15 and 25 percent, according to *The Future of China's Exchange Rate Policy*, a new study by Morris Goldstein and Nicolas Lardy of the Peterson Institute.[13] So this issue is not going to go away.

It could prove a particular problem, especially if high-ranking Chinese officials keep implicitly threatening the United States, raising the possibility of an alternative to the dollar as the world's reserve currency, possibly a basket of currencies or even the renminbi. In the 1980s, Japanese officials attempted to yank Americans' chain in a similar manner. It proved a hollow threat then and, at least in the short run, it is a hollow threat now. For the renminbi to become the reserve currency would require it to be freely traded and Beijing has shown no inclination to do that.

In the meantime, trade frictions are likely to grow. Candidate Obama promised tougher enforcement of U.S. trade laws. In September 2009 the White House imposed restrictions on imports of tires from China, which tripled in volume between 2004 and 2008. Under the terms of China's admission to the WTO, the United States was permitted to limit surging imports of particular products for up to three years to give U.S. manufacturers time to adjust to rising competition.

The Bush administration rejected several different "safeguard" cases relating to imports of other Chinese products, despite findings by the International Trade Commission of injury or threat of injury to U.S. industry. Initially, Beijing reacted quite aggressively, but then quickly toned down the rhetoric, suggesting China sees value in containing bilateral trade tensions.

But American efforts to deal with climate change risk further aggravating trade tensions. U.S. manufacturers worry that if their Chinese competitors do not face comparable costs for controlling emissions of greenhouse gases American companies will be at a competitive disadvantage at home and abroad, worsening the trade deficit. The climate change legislation approved by the U.S. House of Representatives in 2009 included the imposition of duties on carbon-intensive goods shipped from China if Beijing does not make efforts comparable to those in the United States to reduce carbon emissions by 2020. Most observers on Capitol Hill believe some such reciprocity/balance of burdens measure will have to be included in climate legislation if it is to have any chance of final congressional passage.

Obama administration action against China on the trade front is likely to be constrained, given the help Washington needs from Beijing in dealing with Iran, North Korea, and Pakistan. How long this constraint can be sustained remains an open question.

The Foreign Policy Implications

Current U.S. trade policy was shaped by the bitter lessons of the Great Depression. And that protectionism avoidance paradigm was a powerful instrument in extending American influence abroad. Future American trade policy will reflect the lessons of the Great Recession. This realeconomik will have no less of an impact on America's relations with the world.

The willingness of the United States to lower barriers to its market fueled the post-war recoveries of Europe and Japan, cementing their support for U.S. cold war policy. And Washington's support for successive rounds of multilateral trade negotiations successfully spread American beliefs in free markets and democracy.

Throughout this period trade policy was the handmaiden of foreign policy, and domestic economic interests often took a back seat to strategic objectives. In 1960, for example, the State Department allowed Japan to ban imports of foreign cars in an effort to strengthen the Japanese economy to ward off electoral gains by the Japanese Communist Party. The Big Three's dominant share of the Japanese domestic auto market was sacrificed in a decision that came back to haunt Detroit.

Similarly, the strong dollar policy of the Clinton and Bush administrations created a natural market for America's allies, enabling them to run highly-successful export-led growth strategies, reinforcing the peace and stability sought by U.S. foreign policy.

As the United States moves toward a more sustainable international balance sheet there will be unavoidable foreign policy fallout. Recent Canadian and European criticism of U.S. Buy American actions is merely a foretaste of what is to come. The relish exhibited in those attacks suggests the Buy American issue gives U.S. allies an irresistible opportunity to flex their anti-American muscles. Moreover, with every defensive American trade action and every Washington subsidy for a beleaguered industry, nations will complain that the United States is breaking faith with its long-espoused ideals, forsaking its decades-long commitment to free trade and limited government involvement in the economy. To the extent that U.S. actions undermine America's stature as a "city on a hill," U.S. foreign policy could pay a price.

If the United States imports less and China imports more, the Chinese market will cast an ever longer shadow, especially over Asia. If China is no longer simply the last stop on the East Asia supply chain for products headed for the United States, but is rather the region's principle market, South Korea, Taiwan, Malaysia, and others will fall even more into the Chinese economic orbit.

If the crisis and recent experience with trade liberalization lead to a refocusing of U.S. trade policy on two-speed multilateralism and deeper integration with Europe, America could risk forsaking long-term economic and security interests in the fastest-growing, most populous regions in the world. Developing nations, which accounted for 41 percent of global imports in 2007, will consume more than 50 percent of imports by 2025.

And, if Congress continues to refuse to pass the Colombia and South Korea free trade agreements, Washington will forego foreign policy opportunities, even if it does not incur immediate foreign policy costs. Colombia's recent opening of some of its air bases for U.S. anti-drug operations is tangible evidence of the opportunities available for deeper security cooperation that might be enhanced with deeper economic integration, especially in a region where Venezuela, Ecuador, and Nicaragua are not Washington's friends. For its part, South Korea is being inexorably drawn into Beijing's economic sphere of influence through its extensive trade and investment relationship with China. Washington could rue the day it failed to slow that drift.

To the extent that any U.S. current account adjustment is a product of a weaker dollar, foreigners may become less willing to hold assets, to lend money, and to do commercial transactions in dollars, at least at the margin. This may raise new questions about the role of the greenback as a reserve currency, sow doubts about America's long-term superpower status, and erode U.S. leverage in world affairs.

So, the reorientation of U.S. trade policy is not without its potential costs. Nevertheless, it is important to parse the meaningful objections from the background noise. The relative influence of the United States will inexorably decline as the emerging markets of China, India, and others grow. That is a given. But the eclipse of U.S. economic and foreign policy influence is hardly at hand.

Foreigners, including the Chinese, are not dumping dollars. Most publics in most countries still think the United States is the world's leading economic power and do not expect China to supplant America any time soon. International support for the United States has surged, giving the hugely popular Barack Obama political capital to deal with the unavoidable foreign policy friction points created by necessary U.S. economic and trade policy adjustments in the aftermath of the economic crisis.

Many foreign complaints about likely U.S. initiatives in the wake of the economic crisis must be seen for what they are: hypocritical and self-interested. European or Canadian objections to Buy American are truly the pot calling the kettle black, given their own national preference practices. Chinese threats to find an alternative to the dollar ring hollow, as similar Japanese threats did in the 1980s. And Third World opposition to the United States deepening its economic integration with Europe—much as Brazil objected to the Bush administration's free trade in the Americas initiative—reflects their realpolitik understanding that such integration will strengthen the West's hand on a range of issues, from setting technological standards to reinforcing free market norms. In the face of rising Chinese influence in Africa and Latin America, these are not inconsiderable benefits for American economic and foreign policy.

Failure to pass the Colombia free trade agreement has not undermined American stature in Latin America. Anti-Americanism in the region was attributable to other factors over the last eight years. And support for the United States bounced back in 2009, despite there being no prospect for congressional passage of the Colombia deal. There has been a similar rebound in South Korean support for America, despite a similar roadblock on Capitol Hill. South Korean fear of North Korea trumps its frustration with Washington over the free trade agreement.

In any event, an open U.S. market buys less support for America than the U.S. foreign policy establishment would like to believe. Anti-Americanism rose over the last eight years, despite foreigners' growing dependence on the U.S. consumer. In theory, American-led trade liberalization offers great benefits to the developing world. In practice, after eight rounds of global trade negotiations Africa's share of world trade is now less than half of what it was in 1948. Despite U.S. trade preferences extended to Africa in the 1990s, oil and minerals still account for nine-tenths of African exports to the United States, and those come from just three countries. Whatever is done or not done in the world trading system, globalization is no cure-all for the problems of the poor.

At the same time, the foreign policy payoff from a U.S. economy that is once more living within its means and that is no longer the world's largest creditor can not be underestimated. The widespread belief that the out-of-balance U.S. economy has been a negative influence has fueled anti-Americanism in recent years. The image of Secretary of State Hillary Clinton appealing to the Chinese during her first trip to Beijing to buy U.S. bonds lent credence to concerns that dependence on Chinese capital gives Beijing leverage over Washington on a range of issues. Making the U.S. economy stronger and more sustainable will only bolster U.S. foreign policy influence.

The danger of protectionism in the wake of the Great Recession should not be dismissed lightly. Avoiding the mistakes of the past is a high priority. And it is achievable. The American people have not abandoned their faith in trade or free markets. There are no signs that the Obama administration is markedly protectionist. And, while Congress blusters, its trade actions to date have been passively, not actively, restrictive.

Over time, the greater challenge facing the American economy, with the most portentous consequences for U.S. foreign policy, is ensuring a recovery that avoids recreating the global current account imbalances that helped spark the financial crisis. This rebalancing of America's trade relations with the world will undoubtedly cause international friction, leading to calls from the foreign policy community to not rock the boat.   But an American foreign policy built on unsustainable trade imbalances rests on dangerously shifting sands. A new trade/ foreign policy paradigm for a post-crisis world is desperately needed.

Bruce Stokes is the international economics columnist for *National Journal* and a transatlantic fellow at the German Marshall Fund. He is the author of the 2009 Transatlantic Trends Survey published by the German Marshall Fund. He is also coauthor of the 2006 book: *America Against the World: How We Are Different and Why We Are Disliked* (Times Books). A former senior fellow at the Council on Foreign Relations and member of the Council on Foreign Relations, Mr. Stokes was a Japan Society Fellow in 1987 and again in 1989, living in and reporting from Japan. In 2006, Mr. Stokes was honored by the Coalition of Service Industries for his reporting on services issues. In 2004, he was chosen by *International Economy* magazine as one of the most influential China watchers in the American press. In 1995, he was picked by *Washingtonian Magazine* as one of the "Best on Business" reporters in Washington. In 1989, Mr. Stokes won the John Hancock award for excellence in business and economics reporting for his work on Japan. He graduated from the School of Foreign Service at Georgetown University and has an M.A. from The Johns Hopkins School for Advanced International Studies.

[1] "World Trade Report 2009: Trade Policy Commitments and Contingency Measures," World Trade Organization, 2009.

[2] "The Battle of Smoot-Hawley," *The Economist*, 18 December 2008.

[3] Richard Baldwin and Simon Evenett, eds., *The Collapse of Global Trade, Murky Protectionism, and the Crisis: Recommendations for the G20* (Geneva: VoxEU.org Publication, 2009).

[4] "Sarkozy Rolls Out 20bn Euro Rescue Fund," France 24 International News, 20 November 2008, available at http://www.france24.com/en/20081120-sarkozy-unveils-20-billion-euro-sovereign-wealth-fund-france-financial-crisis.

[5] Simon J. Evenett and Bernard Hoekman, "Policy Responses to the Crisis: Implications for the WTO and International Cooperation," Vox EU, 6 July 2009, available at http://www.voxeu.org/index.php?q=node/3738.

[6] "Confidence in Obama Lifts U.S. Image Around the World," a survey of the Pew Global Attitudes Project, released 23 July 2009. Available at http://pewglobal.org/reports/pdf/264.pdf.

[7] "Support for Free Trade Recovers Despite Recession," a survey by the Pew Research Center for the People and the Press, released 28 April 2009, available at http://people-press.org/report/511/free-trade-support-recovers.

[8] Mark Deen and Francine Lacqua, "Trichet Warns World Leaders to Co-Operate or Risk New Crisis," *Irish Independent*, 6 July 2009.

[9] Robert E. Hudec, "The Adequacy of WTO Dispute Settlement Remedies," in *Development, Trade, and the WTO*, ed. Bernard Hoekman, Aaditya Mattoo and Philip English (Washington, DC: World Bank, 2002).

[10] Charles L Schultze and Robert Z. Lawrence, *An American Trade Strategy: Options for the 1990s* (Washington, DC: Brookings Institution Press, 1990).

[11] "The Benefits of Liberalising Product Markets and Reducing Barriers to International Trade and Investment: The Case of the United States and the European Union," Economics Department Working Paper No. 432, Organisation for Economic Co-operation and Development, 26 May 2005.

[12] "Unleashing our Economic Potential: A Primer on the Transatlantic Economic Council," U.S. Chamber of Commerce and BUSINESSEUROPE, 2008.

[13] Morris Goldstein and Nicholas R. Lardy, *The Future of China's Exchange Rate Policy*, (Washington, DC: Peterson Institute: 2009).

"Over the next several years, policymakers will face a balancing act between encouraging a strong and sustained recovery and reducing the fiscal deficit."

— LAURA D. TYSON

Sustaining the Recovery and Containing the Deficit:
A Balancing Act for Policy

Laura D. Tyson
S.K. and Angela Chan Professor of Global Management
Haas School of Business, UC Berkeley

Economic Recovery, Deficits, and Debt: A Domestic Perspective

In the fall of 2008, the U.S. economy was mired in a recession and the world economy was slowing sharply. The recession, which had started in December 2007, gathered momentum and spread around the globe with the bankruptcy of Lehman Brothers and the resulting panic and seizure of global credit markets. By early 2009, the global declines in industrial production, trade, and equity values were tracking declines that had not been experienced since 1929, and economists were warning that the world economy faced another Great Depression. Policymakers in the U.S. and elsewhere confronted two related challenges: how to restore stability to financial markets and how to stem the precipitous and self-reinforcing declines in output and employment. These challenges required the aggressive use of both monetary policy and fiscal policy.

In the U.S., the Federal Reserve slashed interest rates and used innovative "quantitative easing" measures to purchase public and private assets and make loans to the private sector. In the process, the Fed's interest rate fell to zero and the Fed's balance sheet more than doubled. But even unprecedented easing by the Fed was not enough. Providing additional liquidity and loans at near zero interest rates does little to boost spending in a "liquidity trap" situation, in which private investors and consumers are gripped by uncertainty and fear; as they were in late 2008 and early 2009. And the Fed did not have the authority or the resources to provide capital to collapsing financial institutions like AIG, Fannie Mae and Freddie Mac, and Citigroup. Additional spending by the U.S. government was required both to stabilize financial markets and to offset the shortfall in private sector spending that was driving down output at a precipitous rate and destroying millions of jobs. The history of financial crises and recessions shows that their resolution requires sizeable increases in government spending, government deficits, and government debt. The fiscal impact of combating a big financial crisis can be comparable to the fiscal impact of fighting a large war. Current U.S. experience is consistent with this historical record.

In February 2008, Congress passed a $150 billion stimulus package composed mainly of tax cuts. This package did not bolster private sector spending as much as anticipated because households, burdened by debt and falling home prices, devoted a large share of their tax cuts to reducing debt and increasing saving. In November 2008, when credit markets panicked in the aftermath of the Lehman bankruptcy, Congress passed the $700 billion Troubled Asset Relief Program to provide capital to financial institutions teetering on the brink of insolvency. And then, in February 2009, Congress passed a $787 billion stimulus package, the American Recovery and Reinvestment Act (ARRA), amounting to an unprecedented 5.5 percent of GDP. As a result of these two massive programs and the recession itself, which has reduced government revenues and increased government spending on automatic stabilizer programs like unemployment compensation and food stamps, the federal deficit has soared.

According to its most recent projections, the Office of Management and Budget (OMB) estimates the 2009 deficit at $1.5 billion or 11.2 percent of GDP, the largest share since World War II. And the deficit would be much larger but for very low nominal and real interest rates. If the economy had not fallen into recession and if the special stimulus and financial interventions of 2008 and 2009 had not been necessary, the 2009 deficit would be around 3.6 percent of potential or full-employment GDP, far lower than the current deficit, but still sizeable and reflecting the ongoing imbalances inherited from the Bush administration and the previous Congress.[1] Even in the absence of the 2008-2009 recession and the extraordinary fiscal actions required to combat it, the U.S. faced a long-term structural budget problem.

So far, the evidence indicates that the 2009 ARRA has been successful in its goals of bolstering aggregate spending, slowing the pace of the economy's decline, and establishing the conditions for recovery. Private sector forecasters estimate that in the second quarter of 2009, after only $100 billion of the stimulus funds had been injected into the economy, the stimulus added between 2 and 3 percentage points to real GDP growth[2] and about half a million jobs relative to what would have occurred otherwise. At planned spend-out rates of the remaining funds—at about $100 billion per quarter for the five quarters beginning in the fall of 2009—the Council of Economic Advisers forecasts that the output and employment effects will be even larger during the next few quarters.[3] That is in part because the composition of the stimulus spend-out will change from tax incentives and state fiscal relief toward government investments that have larger multiplier effects on output and employment. Private sector forecasters predict that by the end of 2010 the unemployment rate will be almost 2 percentage points lower as a result of the ARRA.[4] The effectiveness of the stimulus package reflects several of its distinguishing features: its size relative to the size of the economy; its timeliness—about three-quarters of the stimulus takes effect within eighteen months, when there is still substantial idle capacity and unemployment; and its composition, with rough balance between tax cuts, support for individuals and state and local governments, and spending on government investments that increase demand and jobs in the short run and increase supply and growth potential over time.

Most economists believe that the U.S. recession ended in the third quarter of 2009. But a self-sustaining recovery is far from a sure thing. And even if it is self-sustaining there are many reasons to believe it will be slow. First, households have lost more than $13 trillion in wealth, they have high levels of debt and debt-service relative to income, and their efforts to repair their balance sheets and increase their saving will constrain a rebound in consumption spending. Second, as in the previous two "jobless" recovery periods in the U.S. economy, output growth is likely to recover well before employment growth. The unemployment rate is likely to remain high for several years, holding down consumer incomes, consumer confidence, and consumer spending. Third, credit is likely to remain tight and expensive for many borrowers as banks continue to deleverage and restore their balance sheets. Tight credit market conditions will be a significant headwind pushing back a strong recovery in private spending. Fourth, a large overhang of residential and commercial property will prevent a strong cyclical recovery in construction. Concerns about these downside risks have led several forecasters to warn about the possibility of a double-dip recession if private sector demand is not strong enough to sustain the economy's growth as fiscal and monetary support measures are removed.

By design, the ARRA is temporary: The stimulus fades away slowly, and by the second half of 2010 it will become a fiscal drag on growth as the rate of change of its spending and tax measures turns negative. Goldman Sachs economists estimate that this drag will amount to 1.3 percent of GDP in 2011. Expiration of some or all of the 2001 and 2003 Bush tax cuts in 2011 as currently scheduled will mean additional fiscal drag in 2011 and 2012.[5] (The Obama administration's budget assumes that these tax cuts will expire for families with incomes in excess of $250,000, while the "Making Work Pay" tax cuts in the stimulus package will be extended through the decade.) If additional actions to reduce projected fiscal deficits are taken, the drag on the economy's growth will be even larger. And if the underlying growth of private demand is not strong enough, the economy could fall back into recession. Concerns about a double-dip recession have a basis in history. The U.S. suffered a double-dip recession in the 1930s, when fiscal policy became overly restrictive in 1937, and Japan suffered a double-dip recession in the 1990s, when fiscal policy became overly restrictive in 1997. According to Alan Auerbach and William Gale, these two experiences show that policymakers err by under-providing fiscal stimulus during major recessionary crises.[6]

Over the next several years, policymakers will face a balancing act between encouraging a strong and sustained recovery and reducing the fiscal deficit. Actions to curb the deficit too soon could push the economy back into recession. But delaying action on the deficit for too long could cause an increase in real long-term interest rates. This would reduce investment and growth and make the deficit problem more difficult to solve. Research indicates that current fiscal deficits do not affect long-term interest rates, but projected deficits do: A recent review of the evidence by William Gale and Peter Orszag finds that each percent increase in projected future deficits raises long-term interest rates by 25 to 50 basis points, and a ten-year deficit that averages 2.5 percent of GDP reduces national saving by 2 to 4 percent and national income by 1 to 2 percent by the end of the period.[7]

The challenge confronting policymakers is made more difficult by the size of the nation's structural budget deficit—or the deficit that would prevail under current policies if the economy were operating at full capacity. According to the most recent (August 2009) OMB projections, the deficit will amount to $9.1 trillion over the next decade, or an average of 5.1 percent of GDP between 2010 and 2019. During this period, the deficit is projected to fall to 3.7 percent in 2018 only to rise back to 4.0 percent in 2019, despite several years of full employment. Overall, the numbers project a structural budget deficit on the order of 4 percent per annum. As a result of persistent deficits, the federal government's debt will continue to grow, climbing to 76.5 percent of GDP by 2019, the highest since 1952. And, by 2019, interest payments on the debt are projected to rise to 3.4 percent of GDP, their highest level to date and higher than the shares of both defense and non-defense discretionary spending in GDP. A significant chunk of these interest payments is owed to foreigners who currently own about half of U.S. Treasury issues. One piece of good news in the OMB projections is that by 2019 the "primary deficit," or the difference between non-interest spending and revenue, is projected to fall to 0.6 percent of GDP; and as the primary deficit falls, the increments to the federal debt decline as well. All of the OMB projections depend on optimistic economic assumptions that a sustained and strong economic recovery takes hold by 2011.

For the reasons discussed below, it is likely that deficits in the 4 to 5 percent range can be financed on reasonable terms and will not pose a threat to the U.S. economy over the next decade. The same cannot be said of the alarming deficits projected further in the future. According to recent estimates by the Center for Budget and Policy Priorities, even without the extraordinary increase in the deficit in 2009, under current spending and tax policies, the annual budget deficit is projected to climb to 21 percent of GDP and the federal debt is projected to hit 279 percent of GDP by 2050, more than two and a half times the previous record at the end of World War II.[8] Gale and Auerbach estimate that the debt-to-GDP level will surpass its 1946 high of 109 percent sometime between 2025 and 2037, and the IMF predicts it will approach 100 percent as early as 2019.[9] Irrespective of differences in economic assumptions, different projections of the long-term deficit and debt reach the same conclusions: The federal budget is on an unsustainable path and the long-term fiscal gap—the immediate and permanent increase in taxes or reduction in spending required to stabilize the debt at its 2009 level as a share of GDP—is significant, amounting at a minimum to about 4 percent of GDP and perhaps to as much as 9 percent.[10]

The main causes of the long-run fiscal problem are growing health care costs and the aging of the population. Together, these factors drive up spending for the three big domestic programs—Medicare, Medicaid, and Social Security. For the past thirty years, costs per beneficiary in the health care system have been growing at about 2 percentage points faster than GDP per capita each year. That's why the Obama administration has focused on health care reform as the key to long-run deficit reduction. But even a significant slowdown in long-term health care costs will leave a sizeable fiscal deficit.

Despite concerns about a high unemployment rate and the possibility of a double-dip recession, concerns about the deficit are already rising among voters, members of Congress, and domestic and foreign investors in U.S. government securities. Voter anxiety is showing up in polls, and congressional anxiety is making it more difficult to agree on a health care reform plan. It already seems likely that the deficit will be an important issue in the 2010 congressional elections. And some investors are already warning about higher long-term interest rates and/or an uptick in inflation caused by government deficits. In particular, the Chinese, who are holding about $1 trillion in dollar-denominated assets, mostly Treasury bills, are warning that they may diversify their holdings and slow down their future purchases because they are worried that U.S. deficits will cause inflation, a decline in the dollar's value, or higher interest rates, all of which will inflict capital losses on their dollar assets. These domestic and foreign concerns about future deficits could be allayed by the passage of a credible plan of spending cuts and revenue increases, scheduled to take effect gradually after the economy has recovered and is operating at—or close to—capacity. By reducing the structural budget deficit in the future, such a plan would ease upward pressure on long-term interest rates, providing a sounder basis for a sustainable recovery. But such a plan would involve painful and politically difficult choices.

The administration's budget projects that non-defense discretionary spending as a share of GDP will fall to near historic lows and that discretionary defense spending as a share of GDP will fall by nearly 2 percentage points over the next decade. It is impossible—and it would be unwise—to make sizeable reductions in the ten-year deficit by making significant cuts in these two areas. Passage of a health care reform bill with credible cost containment features could generate significant savings in projected federal spending on health care, but the administration plans to dedicate these savings to the reform itself over the next ten years, so they would not be available for deficit reduction during this time. Reform that "bends the health care cost line," on the other hand, would have a meaningful effect on longer-run deficits. According to a June 2009 report by the Council of Economic Advisers, if reform reduced the annual growth of health care costs by 1.5 percentage points beginning in 2014, the deficit would be lower by 3 percent of GDP and GDP itself would be 6 percent higher by 2030.[11] Slowing the growth rate of health care costs by smaller amounts—even by as little as 0.5 percent per annum—would have smaller but still significant effects.

With health savings off the table for significant deficit reduction over the next decade, the only other options left are slowing the growth of Social Security and/or increasing revenues. Both are political dynamite and the prospects for meaningful bipartisan agreement in either area are poor. So it is likely that for the next several years the future ten-year deficits will remain as high or go higher than those predicted now. The questions then become: How will the government finance these deficits and at what price? To answer these questions it is necessary to bring the rest of the world into the discussion because foreign investors, in particular foreign governments, have become a major source of lending to the U.S. government.

Economic Recovery, Deficits, and Debt: An International Perspective

In the eight years preceding the global credit crisis, current account imbalances in many nations increased sharply, reaching unprecedented levels. These imbalances had a distinctive pattern—there was a sizeable deterioration in the current account deficits of the United States and a few other developed countries, and there was a dramatic increase in the current account surpluses of China and a few other emerging market countries, including the oil-exporting countries of the Middle East. A current account imbalance is a measure of the gap between national income and domestic demand or between national saving and national investment: A large deficit indicates that a country is spending more than it is producing and has a shortage of national saving; a large surplus indicates that a country is producing more than it is spending and has a surplus of national saving. Between 2000 and 2008, the U.S. saving gap increased dramatically for two reasons. First, largely as a result of policy decisions, the U.S. government budget swung sharply from an average surplus of 1.9 percent of GDP in 2000-2001 to an average deficit of 2.5 percent between 2002 and 2008. Second, and much bigger in its effect on the current account deficit and the borrowing needs of the U.S. economy, net household saving plummeted—the household saving rate fell to zero and residential investment by households soared. As a result of these two developments, the U.S. current account deficit hit 7 percent of GDP by 2007, with the U.S. absorbing about 70 percent of the surplus savings in the rest of the world.[12]

At the same time that U.S. borrowing needs were rising sharply, China and several other countries were generating excess saving and were willing to lend it principally to the U.S. In China, the current account surplus rose from 1.5 percent of GDP to 10 percent of GDP by 2007.[13] The growth of excess saving in China and other countries was so large that despite the increase in U.S. borrowing requirements, real long-term interest rates declined to abnormally low levels by historical standards. Real yields on all fixed income assets, including government bonds, corporate bonds, and securitized debt, fell as the global saving glut sought investment opportunities.[14] Experts estimate that the large flows of foreign capital available to U.S. borrowers reduced interest rates by between 100 and 200 basis points.[15] Without these inflows, the Federal Reserve would not have been able to maintain a low interest rate policy for as long as it did between 2001 and 2004 and the yield curve would not have stayed flat for so long. Low real interest rates and easy financing fueled by foreign saving both encouraged borrowing by U.S. households and the U.S. government and created complacency and growing insensitivity toward risk in global capital markets.

Policy choices played a key role in the growth of excess saving in China and the emerging market countries. In the wake of the 1998-1999 Asian financial crisis, high-saving East Asian economies increased their reliance on exports to fuel growth and amass foreign exchange reserves to protect themselves against future currency and credit crises. China, too, used a variety of policies including generous export subsidies and an undervalued exchange rate, necessitating sustained intervention in currency markets, to promote exports and investments that built additional export capacity. Between 2002 and 2007, China grew at an annual rate of 10.5 percent, China's exports grew at 29 percent a year, and China's investment grew at 24 percent a year. By the end of 2007, exports plus fixed investment rose to 77 percent of GDP in China—a level not seen in any other country, even Japan and Korea during their rapid development years.[16] China was building supply capacity at an astonishing rate and was relying on the U.S. and the rest of the world to provide the demand necessary to keep its supply engine going. And China was financing this demand by lending its excess saving at attractive rates to the U.S. and other countries with saving shortages. When the demand for (and price of) oil rose between 2004 and 2007, the Middle Eastern oil exporting nations also experienced a surge in export income and decided to save rather than spend a large fraction of it, pushing their saving rates to unprecedented levels.[17]

Overall, supply grew much faster than domestic demand in China and several other emerging market nations, and exports to the U.S. and the rest of the world filled the demand gap. The surplus countries relied on the U.S. and the other deficit countries to do some of their spending for them—and provided finance on attractive terms for them to do so. In the words of Martin Wolf, to fuel their export-driven growth, China and other surplus countries relied on deficit countries, especially the U.S., to borrow and spend irresponsibly—to spend to the point of bankruptcy, creating adequate demand to absorb growing global output. As a result of large current account surpluses and large interventions in currency markets to maintain undervalued exchange rates, the surplus countries built huge official foreign exchange reserves, far in excess of anything required to cover future import needs or debt obligations or to provide a buffer against future currency crises. Between 2002 and 2008, as China bought dollars to keep the value of the yuan low, China's foreign exchange reserves grew from almost nothing to $2 trillion. And the risk-averse Chinese authorities responsible for investing these reserves, like the risk-averse public officials responsible for similar investment decisions in other countries, had a strong preference for U.S. government securities, especially low-yielding U.S. Treasury bills. Today, Chinese authorities worry that their low-risk Treasury holdings are subject to sizeable capital losses if the dollar falls, if U.S. inflation ticks up, or if interest rates increase.[18]

As current account surpluses and deficits reached new heights and foreign holdings of U.S. government securities accumulated, many observers warned that they were not sustainable and would result in a crisis in foreign exchange markets or a sudden flight from U.S. dollar assets and a resulting spike in long-term interest rates. Others warned of outbreaks of trade protectionism in response to currency manipulation and import surges from China. As it turned out, the imbalances were indeed unsustainable—they fed an asset bubble that started in the U.S. housing market and flowed through other global debt markets; they fed an investment bubble in export capacity in China and other parts of Asia; they fed an Asian export bubble; and they fed a bubble in oil and other commodity prices. And they resulted in a global credit crisis that sparked a global recession, which in turn has already reduced the imbalances significantly. Despite its severity, the recession has not caused a major shift toward protectionist policies in the U.S. or elsewhere.[19] Nor has the recession caused a flight from the dollar—indeed, initially the dollar rose as investors sought a safe haven from credit market turmoil. Overall, currency markets have remained calm. Despite expressions of concern about the future value of their dollar assets, China and other foreign investors have continued to purchase U.S. government securities on attractive terms; and despite the deterioration in the deficit outlook for the U.S. government, real long-term interest rates have remained low. As of October 2009, the real interest rate paid by the U.S. government on its debt was less than 2 percent.

But what will happen in the future? As the U.S. economy recovers, will the government deficit drive real long-term interest rates up significantly, crowding out private investment and significantly reducing growth and future living standards? Will concerns about the borrowing needs of the U.S. government or concerns about the value of the dollar or U.S. inflation cause a sharp decline in foreign lending to the U.S., igniting a dollar crisis and a spike in interest rates? A recent paper by Fred Bergsten raises these alarm bells and argues that the U.S. government should take deficit-reduction steps sooner rather than later.[20] However, the 2000-2008 experience demonstrates that the relationships between the borrowing needs of the U.S. government, U.S. dependence on inflows of foreign capital, and real long-term interest rates are neither simple nor predictable. Moreover, these relationships are changing in the wake of the 2008 credit crisis and economic slowdown.

Some changes are already apparent, perhaps the most important of which is the increase in the household saving rate in the U.S. Never before and never for so long did U.S. households save as little or borrow as much as they did during the ten years before the crisis. Their extraordinary behavior during this period is not a reliable predictor of their future behavior. As a result of the crisis, U.S. households have lost more than $13 trillion in wealth, and growth in their future incomes will be anemic because of weak employment growth and stagnant wages. The household saving rate has already increased by about 4 percentage points from essentially zero in 2007 to an average of around 4 percent in 2008-2009.[21] Many economists believe the rate will rise further, to the 7 to 10 percent range over the next few years—compared to its long-run average level of 7 percent. U.S. households have begun to reduce their debt levels, but have a long way to go. Given the mountain of debt they face, households are likely to continue to save at a significant rate for the foreseeable future. The increase in household saving has already reduced the U.S. saving gap, and the current account surplus has declined to around 3 percent of GDP. A current account deficit of this magnitude is widely thought to be sustainable over the long term and would stabilize net foreign debt as a share of U.S. GDP. With higher saving by the household sector, the government deficit can grow as a share of GDP even as the current account deficit shrinks and foreign borrowing declines. In essence, American households will cover a larger share of the government's saving gap and foreigners will cover a smaller share. Overall, the U.S. will have higher private saving, lower public saving, and higher national saving relative to GDP.

A sustained reduction in the U.S. current account deficit means that the U.S. will be providing less demand to fuel the global growth engine. If China and other deficit countries do not offset this reduction in demand by increasing their domestic spending and reducing their excess saving, then the world will suffer an even bigger glut of saving and global growth will be considerably slower than it was during the 2000-2008 period. This will make the U.S. recovery more uncertain and the government deficit outlook less favorable. The stronger the growth in demand in the surplus countries, the healthier the global recovery will be. So far, the signals coming from the surplus countries are mixed. China, the largest source of excess saving, has introduced short-term policies that have stimulated consumption spending, but the biggest increases have been in investment spending. And a sustained shift away from reliance on exports to domestic demand will take time and require difficult choices, including an appreciation in the yuan. It will probably take at least three years, more likely five to ten years, for China to fill the global demand void created by a reduction in the U.S. saving gap.[22]

So with American households confronting years of spending restraint to reduce debt and increase saving, with a large number of undercapitalized financial institutions in the U.S., Europe and elsewhere trying to restore balance sheets and restrict lending, and with global growth slow as surplus countries try to substitute domestic demand for export demand, a vigorous global recovery is unlikely. An anemic and difficult recovery marked by de-leveraging, substantial excess capacity relative to potential, a significant risk of a double-dip recession, and continued large fiscal deficits in the U.S. and many other countries is a much more likely outcome. In this environment, real long-term interest rates should remain low, enabling the U.S. government to finance 4 to 5 percent deficits over the next several years at reasonable borrowing rates. But the huge longer-term deficits that are driven primarily by health care costs, the aging of the population, and insufficient tax revenues are not sustainable and pose a serious risk to the U.S. economy. Even before the economy has recovered, the government should commit to a credible plan to gradually address these long-run deficits. Passing such a plan soon would assuage voter and investor anxiety and would reduce upward pressure on interest rates, and the risk of a dollar crisis.

Laura Tyson is the S. K. and Angela Chan Professor of Global Management at the University of California Berkeley. She is also a member of President Obama's Economic Recovery Advisory Board, a Senior Advisor to the McKinsey Global Institute, and the Center for American Progress. Previously, she served as Dean of London Business School from 2002 to 2006, and as Dean of the Haas School of Business, University of California at Berkeley from 1998-2001. She served in the Clinton Administration and was Chair of the President's Council of Economic Advisers from 1993 to 1995 and Chair of the National Economic Council from 1995 to 1996. Dr. Tyson has been a member of the Council on Foreign Relations since 1987, a Director of Morgan Stanley since 1997, a Director of AT&T Inc. since 1999, and a Director of Eastman Kodak since 1997. She earned a B.A. in Economics from Smith College and a Ph.D. in Economics from the Massachusetts Institute of Technology.

[1] William Gale and Alan Auerbach, "An Update on the Economic and Fiscal Crises: 2009 and Beyond," Brookings Institution, Washington, D.C., June 2009.

[2] Joel Prakken, "Is the Stimulus Stimulating?" (presentation at the International Outlook Conference, Washington, D.C., 10 September 2009) and Christina Romer, "So Is It Working? An Assessment of the American Recovery and Reinvestment Act at the Five-Month Mark," (statement at the Economic Club of Washington, Washington, D.C., 6 August 2009).

[3] Romer, "So Is It Working?"

[4] Mark Zandi, "U.S. Fiscal Stimulus Revisited," The Dismal Scientist, 22 June 2009, http://www.economy.com/dismal/article_free.asp?cid=116000&src=msnbc and Prakken, "Is the Stimulus Stimulating?"

[5] Alec Phillips, "The Fiscal Hangover: Hair of the Dog or Cold Turkey?" U.S. Economics Analyst No. 09/33, Goldman Sachs, New York, N.Y., August 2009.

[6] Alan Auerbach and William Gale, "Activist Fiscal Policy to Stabilize Economic Activity," Brookings Institution, Washington, D.C., August 2009.

[7] William Gale and Peter Orszag, "Budget Deficits, National Saving, and Interest Rates," Brookings Institution and Tax Policy Center, Washington, D.C., September 2004.

[8] Kris Cox, James Horney and Richard Kogan, "The Long-Term Fiscal Outlook is Bleak: Restoring Fiscal Sustainability Will Require Major Changes to Programs, Revenues, and the Nation's Health Care System," Center on Budget and Policy Priorities, Washington, D.C., December 2008.

[9] Gale and Auerbach, "An Update on the Economic and Fiscal Crises."

[10] Ibid. and Cox, Horney and Kogan, "The Long-Term Fiscal Outlook."

[11] Council of Economic Advisers, "The Economic Case for Health Care Reform," Washington, D.C., Government Printing Office, June 2009.

[12] Martin Wolf, *Fixing Global Finance* (Baltimore: Johns Hopkins University Press, 2008).

[13] Yu Yongding, "China's Policy Response to Global Economic Crisis and its Perspective on the Reform of the International Monetary System" (paper prepared for the Asia Europe Economic Forum, Kiel, Germany, 7 July 2009).

[14] Kevin Daly and Ben Broadbent, "The Savings Glut, the Return on Capital, and the Rise in Risk Aversion," Global Economics Paper No. 185, Goldman Sachs, New York, N.Y., May 2009.

[15] C. Fred Bergsten, "The Dollar and the Deficits: How Washington Can Prevent the Next Crisis," *Foreign Affairs*, 88, no. 6 (November/December 2009).

[16] Yongding, "China's Policy Response."

[17] Wolf, *Fixing Global Finance*.

[18] Paul Krugman, "China's Dollar Trap," *New York Times*, 2 April 2009; Geoff Dyer, "China's Dollar Dilemma," *Financial Times*, 22 February 2009; and Yongding, "China's Policy Response."

[19] Bruce Stokes, "Rebalancing Economic Engagement: The Foreign Policy Consequences" and Laura D. Tyson, "Collapsing Trade Flows: The Impact on Trade Liberalization," (paper presented at the 61st Plenary Meeting of the Group of Thirty, Banca D'Italia, Rome, 22 May 2009).

[20] Bergsten, "The Dollar and the Deficits."

[21] Richard Berner, "Rising Saving Rate Does Not Signal Renewed Consumer Retrenchment," U.S. Economics Research Report, 13 July 2009.

[22] "Unlocking the Power of Chinese Consumers: An Interview with Stephen Roach," *McKinsey Quarterly*, August 2009.

Part 3

ARE INSTITUTIONS READY FOR
THE CHALLENGE?

CHAPTER 6

Interdependence, Global Issues Management, and Global Economic Governance

Kemal Derviş
Vice President and Director
Global Economy and Development
The Brookings Institution

CHAPTER 7

Picking Up the Pieces:
The Global Crisis and Implications for
U.S. Economic Policymaking

David McCormick
Distinguished Service Professor
Carnegie Mellon University

"The way forward is to build a global system of governance that allows for the management of global issues, the adequate provision of global public goods, and the most effective forms of collective action."

— KEMAL DERVIŞ

Interdependence, Global Issues Management, and Global Economic Governance

Kemal Derviş
Vice President and Director
Global Economy and Development
The Brookings Institution

Introduction

Interdependence among nations and citizens across the world has existed for centuries; the degree of interdependence has increased, however, over the last few decades and has reached unprecedented proportions. The economic crisis of 2008-2009 has further demonstrated how financial products, cross-border credit, trade, and expectations tie the world economy into an interdependent whole. Other forms of interdependence come from carbon emissions, contagious diseases, and nuclear proliferation. No country can address these issues alone. There is need for collective global action that spans many domains and that will have to take many forms.

The way forward is to build a global system of governance that allows for the management of global issues, the adequate provision of global public goods, and the most effective forms of collective action. At the same time, it should be recognized that for decades to come the sovereign nation-state will retain strong legitimacy. Nation-states will remain key legal actors in the international system. Global governance cannot be global government. Instead, it has to be a system involving many different types of international cooperation that facilitates collective action. As U.S. Secretary of State Hillary Clinton recently put it in a speech at the Washington office of the Council on Foreign Relations, we have to move "away from a multipolar world and toward a multi-partner world."[1] This is much easier said than done, however. How to bridge the huge gap between national political space (all politics is local) and the big global issues that must be managed is probably the defining challenge of the twenty-first century.

This paper will focus on several of the economic and financial aspects of global governance, specifically the G-N meetings and the Bretton Woods Institutions. Both have been at the center of attention during the current world crisis.

Different Forms of Economic Governance

Governance takes different forms and works at different levels. It is useful to think of the system of global economic governance as having two tracks—formal and informal.[2] The formal track consists of multilateral institutions established within an international legal framework. This formal system includes a great variety of international agreement-based organizations with special mandates, such as the International Labor Organization (ILO), the International Monetary Fund (IMF), and the World Trade Organization (WTO), to give just three examples. Most of these are part of the loosely connected United Nations system.

The informal track includes meetings of nation-states trying to discuss global or regional issues in an informal setting with the aim of either making some decisions together or of preparing decisions to bring them to the formal governing organs of the treaty-based international organizations. The most prominent of these forums are the "G-N" gatherings that began in the 1970s with the Group of Seven (G-7), and have evolved and grown to the recent two G-20 meetings in Washington and London, with the third of these meetings to be held in Pittsburgh in September of 2009. In the meantime, a "G-8 Plus" recently took place in L'Aquila, Italy on July 8-10, 2009. Although the core of the group was the G-8, it included numerous other countries that attended and participated in various ways, almost demonstrating the demise of the old G-8 in the process. It looks likely that the G-20 meeting that President Obama will host in Pittsburgh in late September will show that the G-20 or a G-20 Plus will supplant the G-7/8 as the foremost international heads of state gathering in the coming years.[3]

Informal Economic Governance

President Valéry Giscard d'Estaing of France conceived of the idea of a G-5 meeting in the mid-1970s and initially planned to invite the U.S., Germany, the UK, and Japan to attend, but ended up inviting Italy as well; the six countries met in Chateau de Rambouillet in November 1975. The following year, former U.S. president Gerald Ford extended an invitation to Canada to join the group in Puerto Rico, and the G-7 was born. Over the three decades since this first meeting, the world has changed dramatically, with parts of the developing world emerging as key actors and shareholders in the world economy. The fact that the meetings have expanded from seven to twenty and more, therefore, is certainly a step in the right direction in terms of enhancing representation, inclusiveness and legitimacy. In reality, the group that met both in Washington and in London was actually larger than the original G-20.[4] Despite this enlargement, and to some degree because of it, it is unclear what the future of these meetings will be. On the one hand, even the enlarged meetings face a problem of legitimacy, with excluded populous countries (such as Egypt and Nigeria, among others) especially unhappy and unwilling to accept their exclusion. On the other hand, the group's expansion has undoubtedly made it more cumbersome. Most observers would agree that significant further expansion would defeat the purpose of having a relatively small number of leaders interact in an informal way that is conducive to debate and discussions. It is important in this context not to forget, however, that the G-20 Plus meetings remain an informal forum. The G-20 Plus is not and cannot be a formal board or decision-making council, such as, for example, the Security Council of the United Nations or the Executive Board of the IMF.

It is the economic crisis of 2008 that led to the convening of the G-20 Plus at the leader level, but the very challenging global issues referred to above will remain and, therefore, so will the need for a global leaders-level meeting. It would be good to institutionalize an annual leaders-level G-20 Plus meeting, even beyond the special economic circumstances of 2008 and 2009.

Despite the problem of size, it should be possible to make these meetings more inclusive. Participation could expand to formally include some rotating representatives of regional groups of smaller and medium-sized countries. After all, the EU has already been present as the twentieth member in the original group; why should it just be the EU? There are several possibilities when it comes to determining the countries representing larger groupings. They could be elected to represent the regional geographical groups at the United Nations, or they could be designated by regional organizations such as the African Union and Association of Southeast Asian Nations (ASEAN), as was done for the London meeting. Apart from including such regional representation, key leaders of multilateral organizations should be present in these meetings: the UN secretary-general, the director-general of the WTO, the managing director of the IMF and the president of the World Bank. Depending on the priorities of a meeting in a particular year, the leaders of other organizations could also be invited. In 2009-2010, for example, employment will likely be a major challenge, and therefore, it would be appropriate to invite the director-general of the ILO. At another time, if there were a particularly serious global health concern, one could expect the director-general of the World Health Organization to participate in the leaders-level forum.

One interesting question relates to regional organizations. Including them, in addition to representatives of regional country groupings, would lead to considerable enlargement of the group and does not appear desirable. The secretary-general of the Organisation for Economic Co-operation and Development may be a special case, if the organization's membership becomes more global in the coming years.

Such participation would lead to having about thirty principals around the table. It would be a group that could deal with key global issues. The inclusion of the heads of the major international organizations would have two advantages: It would be an indirect way of increasing the global legitimacy of these meetings and it would also help to make the meetings more relevant to the actual problem-solving processes for which these organizations have mandates and staff.

Such an enlarged leaders group would remain, however, an informal channel of global economic governance. It should not be treated as a formal governance body. Global governance, resulting in internationally binding decisions, will always come from the formal channel, represented by institutions that function under treaty-based mechanisms. It is within a treaty-based framework that sovereign nation-states can commit themselves to certain policies, dispute resolution mechanisms, or to financial burden sharing arrangements. This does not mean that the informal meetings are redundant. A leaders-level G-20 Plus could have an overall comprehensive perspective on world affairs, provide a unique forum to deal with a broad agenda, and allow key leaders to meet and get to know each other better. One should not ask for more, or expect more, from the informal channel. The more binding forms of global governance must come from the formal channel.

The Bretton Woods Institutions: Key Components of Global Economic Governance

At the end of World War II, the Bretton Woods Institutions (BWIs) were conceived as a central part of formal global economic governance. While they were very broadly placed within the United Nations framework, they de facto operate quite independently from the UN system. There have been periods of great activity and focus on the BWIs, and other periods during which their importance declined. The global economic crisis has again thrust the Bretton Woods Institutions onto center stage, providing a remarkable opportunity to fundamentally reshape the global economic governance architecture in response to the realities of the twenty-first century. Since the Washington and London summits, significant measures have been introduced at a commendable speed. The actions relating to the IMF, in particular, are, however, quite narrowly focused on short-term counters to external shocks. It is imperative that we add to our course of collective action a dimension for long-term functionality of these formal institutions. In this section I will focus on the recent calls for action by the Washington and London G-20 Plus communiqués, progress made, and what is missing for the best way forward.[5]

Reforming the IMF

The last two G-20 Plus meetings have recognized that the IMF (as well as the other formal major multilateral institutions) needs both strengthening and far-reaching reform. This was reflected in the forum's communiqué, which for the IMF supported the following:

- Immediate bilateral financing help of $250 billion from member countries;

- This funding to be folded into an expanded and more flexible borrowing framework (the existing New Agreement to Borrow (NAB) to be increased by up to $500 billion);

- Doubling IMF concessional lending capacity for low-income countries;

- Additional resources from agreed sales of IMF gold to be used to provide $6 billion additional concessional and flexible finance for the poorest countries over the next two to three years;

- New general allocation of special drawing rights (SDRs), equivalent to a $250 billion increase in global reserves;

- Acceleration of the next quota review, to be completed by January 2011.[6]

Progress on this front is being made,[7] especially now that the U.S. Congress has passed measures calling for IMF funding of $100 billion,[8] as well as the vote to move forward with the passing of the Fourth Amendment to the IMF's Articles of Agreement, which allows for a one-time special allocation of SDRs. Japan has also contributed $100 billion and the European Union members are pledging to do the same. Norway, Canada, Switzerland, Korea, Australia, Russia, China, and Brazil have also pledged additional contributions, although China, Russia, and Brazil will buy IMF bonds rather than lend in the NAB framework. India will most likely do the same.[9]

Furthermore, Managing Director Dominique Strauss-Kahn recently shared the IMF's plan to provide close to $8 billion in additional concessional lending made available by the agreed sales of IMF gold (also passed by Congress) as well as the Fund's plan to work on the fourteenth General Review of Quotas and to have completed the review no later than January 2011 (close to two years ahead of schedule).[10]

While these actions are welcome to confront the urgent financial crisis, they are somewhat shortsighted. Private capital flows to emerging market countries have fallen dramatically in the past year and are projected to be close to $700 billion below 2007 levels by the end of the year.[11] The extreme volatility of private capital flows to developing countries over the last two decades and the huge surge in demand for foreign exchange reserves points to the need for both precautionary short-term finance on an ongoing basis and counter-cyclical long-term finance for developing countries. The IMF is viewed as the major source of global precautionary finance. The NAB framework has a provision for repayment after five years, however, and therefore does not necessarily provide permanent availability of precautionary resources for future crises or shocks. In terms of the form precautionary finance is taking, the IMF's newly created Flexible Credit Line (FCL) has features of a truly precautionary facility; however, the conditions for qualification remain vague and should be revised to be clear, non-arbitrary, and broadly acceptable.[12] So far Mexico, Poland, and Colombia have received formal access to this new facility, but it is not clear how broadly the facility will be utilized.

The more effective and sustainable method for the IMF to create sufficient resources for precautionary finance would be through a large up-front quota increase that is followed by regular quota increases. At least part of the quota increases could be linked to additional SDR allocations, gradually turning the SDR into a real and more widely used international reserve asset. The Fourth Amendment recently received the 85 percent majority vote it needed to pass, but it only creates $32 billion in additional SDRs. If, as is likely, the IMF governors approve the $250 billion in additional SDRs recommended in the London communiqué, and hopefully do so prior to the annual IMF meeting in Istanbul in October, it would be a major step in the right direction. Almost two-thirds of the allocations will still go to rich countries, about one-third to emerging economies, and less than 4.5 percent to the less developed countries.

But the provision of sufficient resources is only one of two key problems. The second big issue is the governance of the IMF and the strong desire of the emerging market countries to have a larger say in it. The expedition of the Fund's fourteenth General Review of Quotas by two years is highly welcome, but will not be sufficient in reforming the global economic architecture to secure broad support for the Bretton Woods Institutions. In addition to the resource-augmenting reforms, there is a clear need to reform the relative weight of countries in the governance of the IMF (and the World Bank). The key to progress here is an increase in the weight of the emerging markets and a reduction in the weight of European countries, reflecting the change in the structure of the world economy. Today, Belgium still has greater weight on the Executive Board of the IMF than Brazil—and this is just one example of how reality has overtaken the formal governance structure of the BWIs. Note that the problem is not the weight of the U.S., but the excessive weight and the number of seats of European countries. In this context, the lack of progress in internal cohesion of the European Union translates into a global governance problem.

The World Bank and the RDBs

As discussed above, the IMF is the key international institution for providing short-term financial resources, but there is a clear need for long-term, stable, and counter-cyclical development finance. This need should be fulfilled by the multilateral development bank system—the World Bank and the regional development banks (RDBs). Recapitalization is an immediate need. It is therefore welcome that on April 2, 2009, the G-20 Plus conveners called for "a substantial increase in lending of at least $100 billion by the Multilateral Development Banks (MDBs), including to low-income countries, and ensure that all MDBs have the appropriate capital."[13] The Asian Development Bank has approved a 200 percent general capital increase, as supported by the G-20 Plus, bringing their lender's capital to $165 billion. While these increases in funding are perfectly justified by the short-term urgency to counter the current crisis, there needs to be a clear role for these institutions to provide long-term, effective development finance that better serves low- and middle-income countries.

A "Stability and Growth Facility," along the lines I proposed in 2006, would help serve this purpose.[14] The Facility could be housed at the World Bank, with regional versions of it in the regional development banks, and would serve two main objectives—to provide steady, counter-cyclical, long-term development finance, and to help finance global public goods. The long-term, counter-cyclical activities would protect against the volatility of private capital flows. Furthermore, the terms of at least some loans would be more concessional and accessible to countries suffering from extreme poverty, which does not exist solely in low-income countries. It is important to consider the distribution of global poverty: More than half of the world's poor live in middle-income countries (MICs).[15]

While this fact alone should be compelling enough to include an element of concessionality in these loans, we also need to take into consideration the challenge of financing global public goods. How will our increasingly interdependent world handle climate change and related energy issues, including protection from nuclear proliferation dangers? If countries like Indonesia and Brazil succeed in preserving the rainforest, or if India and China work to produce power with "clean coal" technology, it would directly and positively impact the global community. It is both unreasonable and not feasible for low- and middle-income countries to bear all such global public goods-related costs. The fight against climate change and the provision of other global public goods requires global access to long-term development finance at an affordable cost. This is another powerful reason for strengthening the World Bank and the MDB system and allowing some "blending" of concessional resources with commercial funds.

The United Nations and the Economic and Social Domain

While the Bretton Woods Institutions are formally part of the UN system, they are quite independent in their operations. Apart from a vague reference in the UN Charter to the Economic and Social Council (ECOSOC) as an overall coordinating body, there is, in reality, nothing tying the World Bank or the IMF to the UN system. On the other hand, the UN is active in the economic domain, both intellectually and operationally.

There are two opposing views on the relationship between the UN and the Bretton Woods Institutions. One view argues that the UN should act as an overarching, coordinating and legitimizing body. Those holding this view also see a continuing and strong role for the UN's various development organizations, including the United Nations Development Programme (UNDP) and the Department of Economic and Social Affairs (DESA). Others argue that the overlapping and often competing roles of the UN system and the Bretton Woods Institutions are undesirable. They argue that the BWIs and the regional development banks are sufficient for the economic and social domain. Those holding this second view would focus the UN system more narrowly on political matters, peacekeeping, and humanitarian crisis response.

There is little doubt that the UN has a great deal of legitimacy around the world, as demonstrated in numerous opinion polls. Somewhat surprisingly, this is true—to varying degrees, depending on the year—even in the United States. This legitimacy is rooted in the UN's universality, the nature of its Charter, and perhaps also in the role many secretaries-general have played in peacebuilding and advocacy for humanitarian and environmental causes. The fact that the secretary-general can come from any country in the world may be another explanatory factor. In contrast, the Bretton Woods Institutions have been and are still being perceived as instruments of the rich countries, often "imposing" tough economic and fiscal conditions on developing countries, without the ability to also supervise the rich countries' policies. The recent financial sector excesses in the rich countries have again demonstrated this asymmetry. The U.S., for example, never agreed to the kind of financial sector assessment that the IMF and the World Bank carried out for developing countries. At the same time, the Bretton Woods Institutions are widely considered to have extremely professional and qualified staff. They are generally considered, even by many of their critics, to be efficient institutions. Historically, they have also had—even before the ongoing augmentations triggered by the crisis—much larger resources than other UN organizations.

The crisis of 2008-2009, the rise of many emerging market economies, the great increase in the weight of China and India in the world economy, and the increasing interdependence of nations referred to in the beginning of this paper, have all been factors leading to fundamental changes that will affect the interface between the United Nations and the Bretton Woods Institutions. The transformation of the G-8 into the G-20 Plus is a reflection of these irreversible structural changes. The international community will now have to address more explicitly the respective roles of the BWIs and the United Nations system. Instead of the Bretton Woods Institutions "belonging" to the U.S. and Europe (as well as Japan) and the UN economic and social organizations "belonging" to the developing countries because of the sheer weight of their numbers in the General Assembly, the G-20 meetings and the dynamics of governance reform at the BWIs point towards a new era when it may be possible to organize the work of the entire system more rationally and efficiently. It is quite clear, for example, that next time around the president of the World Bank and the managing director of the IMF will not necessarily be an American and a European. Both the U.S. and Europe have, implicitly at least, agreed to a more open selection process. By the middle of the next decade, there is little doubt that the weight of China, India, Brazil, and other emerging market countries will have substantially increased in the governing organs of the BWIs. This could and should reinforce the legitimacy of these institutions and strengthen their ability to contribute to regulating the world economy, provided that the traditional developed countries accept such a role for the emerging markets. If this is allowed to happen, there will be less of a perceived "legitimacy contrast" between the UN and the Bretton Woods Institutions, and cooperation could be organized based on non-duplication and efficiency considerations, rather than being driven by political cleavages and the North-South divide. This could lead to more coherent global economic governance and greater effectiveness in the use of resources, the fight against poverty, and the management of global collective action.

Kemal Derviş is the Vice President and Director of Global Economy and Development at the Brookings Institution. Previously, he served as Administrator of the United Nations Development Programme and Chair of the United Nations Development Group. Prior to his appointment with UNDP, Dr. Dervis was a member of the Turkish Parliament representing Istanbul, from November 2002 to June 2005. During this time, he represented the Turkish Parliament in the Constitutional Convention on the Future of Europe and was a member of the joint commission of the Turkish and European Parliaments. He was also active in the Economics and Foreign Policy Forum, a Turkish NGO working on economic and political issues. From March 2001 to August 2002, Dr. Dervis was Minister for Economic Affairs and the Treasury of the Republic of Turkey, responsible for Turkey's recovery program after the devastating financial crisis that hit the country in February 2001. Dr. Dervis has also served at the World Bank, where he held various positions including Vice-President for Poverty Reduction and Economic Management, from 2000-2001; Vice-President for the Middle East and North Africa Region, from 1996-2000; Division Chief for Industrial and Trade Strategy, and Director for the Central Europe Department after the fall of the Berlin Wall. Dr. Dervis earned a B.A. and master's degrees from the London School of Economics and a Ph.D. from Princeton University.

[1] Secretary of State Hillary Clinton, "Foreign Policy Address at the Council on Foreign Relations" (speech, Council on Foreign Relations, Washington, D.C., 15 July 2009). The speech is available at http://www.state.gov/secretary/rm/2009a/july/126071.htm.

[2] This distinction between formal and informal governance follows the discussion in Kemal Dervis, "A Way Forward: Formal and Informal Aspects of Economic Governance," in *Re-Defining the Global Economy*, Friedrich Ebert Stiftung Occasional Paper, (New York, April 2009), 42.

[3] The informal track also includes meetings and interactions between non-government actors, which have become increasingly important, but this sub-track will not be the focus of this paper.

[4] The London meeting actually included the G-20 members as well as Spain, the Netherlands, the chairs of the New Partnership for Africa's Development, the Association of Southeast Asian Nations and the African Union Commission, as well as the secretary-general of the UN, the director-general of the WTO, the president of the World Bank, and the managing director of the IMF.

[5] A very important part of formal economic governance is, of course, the successor to the GATT—the WTO. But the WTO has not been the focus of international meetings in 2008-2009, partly because of the stalemate in the Doha Round trade negotiations and partly because it is the financial sector and macroeconomic issues that have been pushed to the forefront by the worldwide crisis. I will not discuss trade issues or the WTO in this paper.

[6] "The Global Plan for Recovery and Reform, Annex: Declaration on Delivering Resources through the International Financial Institutions" (official communiqué issued at the close of the G20 London Summit, London, UK, 2 April 2009), available at http://www.number10.gov.uk/Page18930.

[7] Japan has made a $100 billion borrowing agreement, Norway $4.5 billion, Canada $10 billion, Switzerland $10 billion, and pledges from the European Union members amount to approximately $100 billion. For more information, see the IMF website (www.imf.org).

[8] Critical for IMF reform, as several measures need an 85 percent majority voting approval, and the United States has a voting power of 16.77 percent. "Fund Income and Expenditure: Board Backs Plan to Adopt New Income Model for IMF," International Monetary Fund, http://www.imf.org/external/pubs/ft/survey/so/2008/NEW040708A.htm.

[9] "Bolstering the IMF's Lending Capacity," International Monetary Fund, http://www.imf.org/external/np/exr/faq/contribution.htm.

[10] "IMF Asked to Aid G-8 with Exit Strategies for Crisis Policies," International Monetary Fund, 13 June 2009, http://www.imf.org/external/pubs/ft/survey/so/2009/new061309a.htm.

[11] "Capital Flows to Emerging Market Economies," Institute for International Finance, 27 January 2009. Available on the IIF's website (www.iif.com).

[12] For a more elaborate treatment of the challenges involved in providing the world with sufficient amounts of precautionary finance, see Kemal Dervis, "Precautionary Resources and Long Term Development Finance: The Financial Role of the Bretton Woods Institutions after the Crisis" (paper prepared for the Center for Global Development's Richard H. Sabot Lecture, Washington, D.C., 11 June 2009).

[13] "The Global Plan for Recovery and Reform," (official communiqué issued at the close of the G20 London Summit, London, UK, 2 April 2009), available at http://www.g20.org/Documents/final-communique.pdf.

[14] See Kemal Derviş and Nancy Birdsall, "A Stability and Social Investment Facility for High-Debt Countries," in *Reforming the IMF for the 21st Century*, ed. Edwin M. Truman (Washington, D.C.: Peterson Institute for International Economics, 2006).

[15] Those living below the poverty line are defined as people who earn less than $2 per day. "Middle Income Countries," The World Bank, http://web.worldbank.org/WBSITE/EXTERNAL/PROJECTS/0,,contentMDK:20976054~pagePK:41367~piPK:51533~theSitePK:40941,00.html.

"Equally important, however, is retooling international economic policymaking to ensure the United States is effective across a dizzying array of economic policy issues in a rapidly changing and increasingly complicated world."

—DAVID MCCORMICK

Picking Up the Pieces:
The Global Crisis and Implications for U.S. Economic Policymaking

David McCormick
Distinguished Service Professor
Carnegie Mellon University

If the previous twenty years were to be described as the childhood phase in the development of globalization, the current phase and the decade ahead are likely to be more akin to the adolescence phase and all that implies in terms of uncertainty, volatility, and difficulty for economic policymakers. We are in the midst of an economic crisis unprecedented in modern times, and the policy steps that have been and will be taken have enormous implications for the global economy, U.S. national security, and America's place in the world.

While it is still too early to understand fully all that has transpired in the past twenty-four months, some implications for U.S. economic policymakers and institutions are beginning to come into focus. This chapter is organized into four sections. It begins by describing the near-term challenge of responding to the crisis as well as the consequences of the actions already taken. Specifically, it highlights clear lessons about the capabilities the United States must develop in order to better manage the consequences of the actions already taken, improve coordination with international allies on current and future policy actions, and ensure the regulatory system is reformed to guard against such crises in the future.

Second, this paper chronicles the "new reality" in terms of the challenges to globalization resulting from the economic crisis, and describes the constraints that policymakers will confront in leading and influencing in the international economic arena. In the third section, the paper discusses an array of longer-term economic priorities—more pressing than ever as a consequence of the crisis—which require focused leadership and adequate resources to advance U.S. interests. The final section examines the need to reshape international economic policymaking within the United States to ensure that we may more effectively manage and lead the international economic agenda in a rapidly changing and increasingly complicated world.

The Near-Term Challenge: Crisis Response and Reconciliation

As the crisis worsened throughout 2008 with a speed and breadth that quickly surpassed even "worst case scenario" planning, U.S. policymakers were forced to act creatively, in ways that often pushed the envelope of their statutory authority and revealed fundamental shortcomings in the capabilities of U.S. economic institutions. These dramatic actions have created a whole new set of responsibilities and challenges in managing, and—wherever appropriate—undoing, these government interventions over time. Today's economic policymaking apparatus is inadequate and must be transformed to accommodate these new and demanding responsibilities.

Pulling Back from the Abyss

In mid-October 2008, as credit markets froze, equity markets posted unprecedented declines, and many financial institutions teetered on the brink of failure, U.S. authorities—in concert with policymakers around the world—rolled out a comprehensive plan, the economic equivalent of the Powell Doctrine, of using overwhelming force to stabilize the system.

First, going beyond traditional monetary policy and the direct interventions it had made in facilitating the sale of Bear Stearns to J.P. Morgan and providing liquidity to American International Group (AIG), the Federal Reserve launched a broad range of liquidity facilities to increase access to funding for all sectors of the economy. In addition, the Federal Reserve committed to purchasing up to $1.8 trillion of government-sponsored enterprise (GSE) debt, GSE mortgage-backed securities, and Treasuries to lower interest rates and stimulate the housing market, thus expanding its balance sheet to historic levels.

Second, with the support of the Treasury and the Federal Reserve, the Federal Deposit Insurance Corporation (FDIC) launched a program to guarantee newly-issued debt of participating FDIC-insured financial institutions for up to three years, as well as deposits in non-interest bearing deposit transaction accounts. These actions to mitigate counterparty risk and avert destabilizing flows of capital between U.S. banks were meant to prevent a run on our banks, a scenario which seemed very plausible at the time.

Third, and perhaps most important, the Treasury provided much-needed capital to address a root cause of the crisis, the buildup of illiquid mortgage-related assets on the balance sheets of financial institutions. Under authority granted by Congress, Treasury designed a capital injection plan, financed through what became known as the Troubled Asset Relief Program (TARP), to strengthen and stabilize the financial system. Secretary Tim Geithner followed up on this plan in April 2009 by creating a public-private partnership through which the private sector would purchase legacy assets from the balance sheets of U.S. financial institutions, thereby allowing them to more easily raise private capital. This authority has also been used to finance turnaround plans for AIG, General Motors, and Chrysler, among others.

Finally, the U.S. government acted quickly to invigorate the economy through government spending. Following on the $150 billion bipartisan stimulus package put in place by the Bush administration in 2008, the Obama administration is in the process of implementing a $787 billion stimulus to offset the dramatic decline in the U.S. economy.

The efficacy of these efforts will undoubtedly be debated for years to come. For example, critics point to the failure of the government to intervene to prevent the fall of Lehman Brothers as a turning point (those who were in government at the time argue that there was an absence of authority to do so). Moreover, in retrospect, there is little doubt that policymakers misjudged the speed and severity of the crisis at every step, and as a consequence their public communications along the way were often piecemeal and incomplete and sometimes undermined market confidence. Perhaps such shortcomings are inevitable when responding to the uncertainty and urgency that are the trademarks of any crisis of such magnitude. With the benefit of time historians will have the opportunity to sort through these questions. There is little doubt, however, that in its totality, this massive intervention has had the desired effect: The risk of a depression-like downturn or financial market meltdown seems increasingly remote, even as the longer-term outlook remains uncertain.

But left undone is the work of determining how these massive government interventions are to be managed to ensure they are effective, transparent, and, perhaps most important, fade away over time. This is a multi-year, perhaps multi-decade, challenge, and the Federal Reserve, the Treasury, and other parts of the U.S. government are understaffed and unprepared for this long-term challenge. While there is insufficient space to address this issue in much detail, a few areas deserve brief mention.

First, the U.S. Treasury is now one of the biggest asset managers in the world, with investments or obligations of over $600 billion in programs supporting over six hundred private sector institutions including General Motors, AIG and Citigroup. The Office of Financial Stability, created by Congress in the fall of 2008, built an organization of over 170 professionals in a few short months, but is still insufficient to oversee and exit from these investments.[1]

Recommendation 1: Congress and the administration should ensure that Treasury's Office of Financial Stability has the appropriate resources and subject matter expertise to carry out this critical mission in the years ahead.

To provide the certainty necessary for investors and market participants, the administration will also need to provide clear and consistent guidelines for how and when they will engage with these private sector institutions in which the government has ownership interest, and the degree to which it will seek to influence how they are managed. For example, to what extent are issues like compensation policies, marketing activities, customer events, capital expenditures, and governance processes the purview of the government? There are no easy answers, but there is enormous potential for expanding government involvement and the politicization of management decisions with devastating long-term implications for the health of the private sector.

Recommendation 2: The administration should carefully proscribe and limit government involvement in these enterprises while setting clear timelines and processes for exiting government investments as soon as possible.

The Federal Reserve has been enormously creative and effective at responding to the crisis with a unique blend of policy tools that has allowed it to lend directly to individual institutions, provide liquidity directly to credit markets, and buy longer-term securities or Treasuries to stabilize interest rates. But this flurry of activity has stretched thin the Federal Reserve and its dedicated staff. Thus, a key question is how to best manage these many programs and investments going forward while shrinking the Fed's balance sheet as quickly as possible and minimizing the potential for inflation.

Recommendation 3: The Federal Reserve, working in concert with the Congress and the administration, must acquire new skills and perhaps implement needed changes to its organizational model to help overcome these challenges.

Regardless of one's view on the content of the stimulus, it is critical to the economic recovery that the $787 billion in stimulus be disbursed in an effective and expeditious manner. This means ensuring these resources are directed only to projects consistent with the intent of Congress and the administration and implemented fully over the next twenty-four months. To date, only $110 billion, or 14 percent, of the stimulus has been spent, well behind some initial forecasts.[2] To accelerate this effort, the Obama administration has established a dedicated office in the Office of Management and Budget and identified a senior official with singular accountability for overseeing the effective disbursement of stimulus dollars.

Recommendation 4: The administration must ensure that its efforts to manage and oversee the implementation of the stimulus legislation, so critical to the pace and strength of the recovery, remain a top priority and are adequately resourced.

Multilateral Engagement: Pursuing U.S. Interests through the G-20

In recent months, multilateral engagement has become synonymous with the Group of 20 (G-20), which has come to serve as the coordinating body for the global response to the economic crisis. In the fall of 2008, President George Bush and Treasury Secretary Henry Paulson launched the G-20 leaders process with the intent of developing consensus on the root causes of the crisis, creating a common framework for policy responses, and beginning the process of reforming regulations across the major economies to address shortcomings that contributed to the crisis.

To the surprise of many, the G-20 leaders meetings in Washington in November 2008 and London in April 2009 achieved tangible results by providing common principles to guide the crisis response, committing to increased resources for and needed governance changes in international financial institutions like the International Monetary Fund (IMF) and the World Bank as well as global regulatory bodies like the Financial Stability Board and the Bank for International Settlements (BIS). In addition, the G-20 agreed on detailed reforms of the financial system to strengthen transparency and accountability, improve risk management, and promote market integrity. Certainly, the G-20 might have been bolder by dealing head-on with the issue of global imbalances, which contributed to the crisis, or acting in concert with ambitious stimulus spending. But, to date, the G-20 has taken tangible and important steps, established an ambitious path forward, and far exceeded the expectations of most of the participants.

Yet the G-20's credibility going forward will depend on its ability to transition from encouraging words to effective coordinated action. Subtly influencing this effort will be a key challenge and opportunity for U.S. policymakers. For example, there will be inevitable difficulties implementing many of the agreements already reached by the G-20. Further, the G-20 is unwieldy to manage and many participants are inexperienced in operating in a forum with such a meaty policy agenda, so member countries must be willing to dedicate resources and establish rigorous processes to refine consensus proposals and oversee their implementation. While there is a growing consensus that the G-8 is not an appropriately representative forum for tackling many global challenges, opinions are divided on whether the G-20 or some smaller group should take its place. This question is best left unanswered for the time being as it is politically sensitive, distracting, and may well answer itself with the passage of time. Moreover, the G-20 leaders have already committed themselves to a robust gameplan for addressing the crisis; therefore, the focus should be on ensuring that effort is successful.

For the foreseeable future, U.S. policymakers must consider how best to advance their agenda within each of these respective dialogues and ensure they receive the needed resources and required focus. For example, should climate change be a topic addressed in the agenda of the G-20, the G-8, the Major Economies Process launched by the Bush administration, or all three? How can disparate regulators in the United States like the Federal Reserve and the FDIC be best coordinated to ensure a unified position on the critical regulatory reform issues under discussion in these international fora? Given the expanding role of the international financial institutions, what steps should the executive branch take to ensure continued support on Capitol Hill and adequate influence as the leading shareholder within these institutions?

Recommendation 5: The administration should develop a comprehensive plan for advancing its agenda and ensuring unified and effective U.S. positions across a broad and expanding array of international dialogues.

The Regulatory Reform Agenda

The financial crisis also confirmed the need for dramatic reform of the U.S. regulatory system. This reform imperative is most evident in the failure of the U.S. regulatory system to foresee and mitigate the buildup of systemic risk in our financial markets and the inability of economic policymakers and institutions to effectively respond to the resulting crisis due to insufficient authority and unclear mandates.

Regulatory reform efforts began in early 2008, when the United States began to implement the specific findings of international and domestic expert groups to improve transparency, prudential regulation, risk management, and market discipline. In March 2008, Secretary Paulson released a blueprint for a modernized financial regulatory structure that called for dramatic consolidation of the existing bloated regulatory structure. Building on this, the Obama administration released its detailed regulatory reform plan in June 2009. While there is debate over whether this proposal goes too far in some areas (a separate consumer regulator) and not far enough in others (the failure to consolidate existing regulatory bodies), it addresses head-on three critical issues.

First, the proposal tackles the issue of systemic risk by granting the Federal Reserve the power to supervise all large financial institutions that pose systemic risk, even those that do not own banks. These large interconnected firms would be subject to heightened capital, liquidity, and risk management standards. The Federal Reserve's efforts would be aided by a new Financial Services Oversight Council comprised of other regulators with the power to gather information from any firm to identify emerging systemic risks.

Second, the proposal provides the Department of the Treasury with resolution authority over non-bank financial institutions that pose systemic risk. This authority, akin to the FDIC's capacity to oversee the wind-down of insolvent FDIC-insured institutions, would provide the Treasury with the ability to manage the orderly resolution of insolvent institutions such as Lehman Brothers, thereby avoiding the destabilizing effects felt in September 2008.

Third, the administration has proposed reforms to promote greater efficiency, transparency, and regulatory oversight in the over-the-counter derivatives market. While there is ongoing debate about the degree to which these reforms should include non-standard derivatives contracts, these proposals go a long way toward addressing an enormous, opaque, and potentially risky component of modern financial markets.

This reform plan is consistent with the broad international principles agreed to by the G-20. And despite a great deal of political posturing by a number of European leaders, America's reform agenda is more defined and further advanced than those of its European counterparts. In turning this ambitious reform agenda into reality, policymakers must undertake focused efforts in several areas:

Recommendation 6: The administration should: (a) work with Congress to ensure regulatory reform legislation is implemented as soon as possible before the political momentum for difficult actions ebbs and that the Federal Reserve and Treasury are provided the resources needed to implement their new responsibilities; and (b) guard against other countries or international regulatory bodies pursuing international standards that go beyond or are inconsistent with these rigorous reforms.

The New Reality: Challenges for Globalization

The financial crisis has brought new intensity to the debate over the inherent benefits and challenges of growing economic interdependence and connectivity. Globalization has historically been defined by the increasing dispersion of global economic power, with the industrialized world accounting for a shrinking portion of the world economy and emerging markets increasingly driving its growth. Among industrialized economies, the United States, which represents 25 percent of the world economy, has stood out as a rare example of a dynamic free market economy, with growth of 63 percent from 1998 to 2008, accounting for roughly one-fifth of global growth during that same period. While the trade and capital flows and the productivity improvements resulting from economic and technological integration have brought significant net benefits, they have also introduced vulnerabilities, ranging from the H1N1 virus to global climate change.

The global financial crisis has altered, permanently perhaps, some of the underlying dynamics of globalization and caused some in the United States and around the world to reconsider the balance of its benefits and costs. These changes are evident in multiple areas. First, while the need for American leadership during this period is more pressing than ever, its capacity to do so is diminished as the financial crisis marks the passing of a "unipolar moment" for the world economy. Even if the U.S. economy returns to growth in the coming quarters, it is unlikely that it will return to the position in the world it enjoyed in the decade past.[4] This economic weakness undermines America's authority, feeds growing skepticism over the wisdom of lightly regulated, market-based decision-making, and tests U.S. credibility at a time when budgetary shortfalls constrain financial support for foreign assistance, international security, and diplomacy.

Second, as the crisis has evolved, key emerging market countries such as China, India, and Brazil have gained relative influence more quickly than they expected and perhaps even wanted. The influence results not only from the fact that they comprise an even greater part of the global economy than ever before and are the locus of most of the growth in the global economy, but also because they have largely sidestepped many of the problems suffered in the financial markets of the West, and in the case of China, are a critical source of financing for the enormous levels of debt being issued by the United States and other Western economies.

Third, the crisis has altered domestic politics and perceptions within countries. While the emerging markets have been remarkably resilient, many developing countries have suffered dramatically, exacerbating poverty and destabilizing political conditions in countries ranging from Latvia to Pakistan. Growing economic pressures are also contributing to rising protectionism in the form of trade barriers, export subsidies, capital restrictions, buy-local constraints, and heightened rhetoric in many developing and industrialized countries, including the United States.

These views are reflected in Congress, where the benefits of trade and foreign investment are openly questioned by members from across the political spectrum. They are manifest in the restrictions on visas for highly skilled workers and "Buy American" provisions of the stimulus bill and visible in the tariff provisions in the recent House climate bill. Most disappointing, many of these steps have been taken in the U.S. and elsewhere following the uniform commitment by all the G-20 leaders in November 2008 to push back on the forces of protectionism. The Obama administration is uniquely positioned to influence this important debate with words and deeds, but thus far has not made combating these misguided policies at home and promoting an ambitious free trade and open investment agenda abroad a priority.

Longer-Term Priorities: Moving Beyond the Crisis

These shifts in the dynamics of economic power pose unique challenges and constraints as well as some opportunities for U.S. efforts to stabilize the global economy and support long-term economic integration and prosperity. Beyond the targeted, crisis-related policy responses outlined earlier, actions needed to maintain U.S. leadership on the international economic agenda in the longer run fall into several important categories.

Promoting U.S. Competitiveness

The crisis has revealed a need for the United States to transform its economy into one that is less dependent on consumption, less susceptible to bubbles, and built on more diverse, dynamic sources of growth. It will also require policymakers to bring about substantive changes on less complicated but politically sticky issues such as immigration policy and export controls, which are currently drags on innovation and growth, particularly in the high technology sector. At a time when its economy is under enormous pressure, the United States cannot afford to restrict the entry of highly skilled immigrants and talented entrepreneurs who will create jobs and bring investment, or to restrict the export of commercially available technology to the fastest growing markets in the world.

Advancing Free Trade and Open Investment

The protectionist fears described earlier are symptomatic of the anxieties created by the financial crisis and a rapidly changing world. But, the free flow of trade, investment, and intellectual capital to the United States is more of a cure for U.S. economic challenges than a cause and therefore must be central to America's international economic policy going forward. In 2007, for example, exports accounted for 12 percent of U.S. gross domestic product (GDP) and contributed to more than a third of U.S. economic growth.[5] Likewise, over five million jobs in the United States are directly created by foreign direct investment (FDI) and an additional five million jobs are indirectly supported by the U.S. operations of foreign-owned firms.[6]

Policymakers must unflinchingly maintain their commitment to free trade and open investment while also recognizing and addressing the potential disruptions resulting from them. As examples, the United States must take the lead in implementing existing free trade agreements with countries like Panama, Colombia, and South Korea and take steps to conclude the Doha multilateral trade round that liberalizes goods and especially services, a key strength of the

U.S. economy. Equally important, however, Congress and the administration must work to design more effective policies and approaches for helping individuals, companies, and regions adapt to the rapid pace of global economic change by providing new training, new skills, and a new model for assisting those displaced by the dynamics of global engagement—current policies are a hodgepodge created since the Kennedy administration that calls out for systematic reform.[7]

Addressing Global Sustainability

The financial crisis has also created an increasingly complicated environment for action on global issues such as climate change, HIV/AIDS, and poverty, all of which pose enormous risks for economic growth as well as threats to U.S. national security. Policymakers will face the dual task of coordinating and directing U.S. efforts internationally while crafting domestic policy responses that reflect very real political and budgetary constraints.

As the crisis has evolved, international financial institutions have been instrumental in addressing these collective challenges and in considering new tools and priorities. The IMF has developed creative programs to help strong-performing economies confront temporary liquidity problems, for example, and the World Bank has championed efforts to address food and energy needs, develop innovative ways to strengthen country financial sectors, and address potential shortfalls in trade finance. However, these institutions will be most effective when they engage on issues most consistent with their comparative advantages. They must therefore carefully align their activities with one another and with other donors and ensure that assistance is effectively targeted and used more efficiently.

Given that these institutions will play an important and expanding role for the foreseeable future, Congress and the administration will need to be more active in assuring that these institutions have the necessary resources to carry out their changing missions, move forward on much delayed governance reforms, and execute their missions in a way that advances global and U.S. interests. This will also require the administration to educate Congress and the general public on the important role of these institutions and to provide sufficient resources and leadership focus within the White House, Treasury, and the State Department to play an active hand in this critical agenda.

Responding to the New Reality: Retooling International Economic Policymaking

As the dust settles after more than a year of "crisis response," it is important to step back and rethink and reform the economic policymaking apparatus. As described earlier, this should include building capabilities to effectively manage, and ultimately exit, the enormous government interventions that have taken place in recent months. Equally important, however, is retooling international economic policymaking to ensure the United States is effective across a dizzying array of economic policy issues in a rapidly changing and increasingly complicated world. Several specific areas warrant brief mention and some suggestions.

First, as the international economic landscape grows in complexity, it is no longer clear that the existing economic institutions are appropriate in design or mandate to accommodate these new challenges. For example, in designing policies to combat global climate change, a plethora of agencies including the Departments of State, Energy, Commerce, and Treasury, not to mention the Council on Environmental Quality, the United States Trade Representative, and the Securities and Exchange Commission all have significant interests and responsibilities in this area. Yet is this array of institutions, even when ably coordinated, appropriate or capable of developing and executing the needed policy changes? The same might be asked in the area of foreign assistance, where the U.S. Agency for International Development, the Millennium Challenge Corporation, the Overseas Private Investment Corporation, and the Department of Defense all perform valuable roles, but may at times lack common purpose and adequate collaboration in pursuing their organizational missions.

Recommendation 7: The administration should undertake a strategic review of the mandates and responsibilities of its economic institutions in light of pressing international economic issues such as global climate change and foreign assistance that may require new capabilities and consolidated accountability within the executive branch of government.

Second, even if one assumes that the existing agencies are up to the challenge, there is little doubt that today's environment demands even greater integration of domestic and foreign policy and more effective policy coordination within the White House. Measured policy decisions, for example, on difficult issues ranging from the trade agenda to development policy, immigration policy, export controls, and climate change will require extensive coordination by the National Economic Council and National Security Council across a number of critical agencies and constituencies. That the international economic affairs portfolio has a seat at the table is an important first step, but more must be done. The current structure within the White House supporting international economic policy is far from optimal in meeting these new and growing demands.

For example, in recent years there has been a proliferation of "deputies" within the National Security Council, with the deputy national security advisor for international economic affairs serving as one of many senior officials in the NSC. Likewise, the international economic agenda is one of many "issues areas" too often lost in the vast array of pressing foreign policy issues confronting any administration. A successful model to emulate is the President's Working Group (PWG), chaired by the Treasury secretary and composed of key regulators from across the government. The PWG has played a valuable role in ensuring communication and coordination across the convoluted U.S. regulatory structure on the domestic and international regulatory agenda, and this need is only likely to grow in the future.

Recommendation 8: The administration should contemplate the creation and regular meeting of a cabinet-level International Economics Committee of Principals (somewhat akin to the National Security Council); elevate the role of deputy national security advisor for international economic affairs to ensure steady focus and continued progress on these difficult issues; and raise the profile of the PWG as the critical body for ensuring alignment among all parties on the regulatory agenda and coherent, consistent positions in negotiations with other international bodies.[7]

Third, because of the prominence of international economic issues and their importance to broader U.S. foreign policy objectives, significant changes in how the government structures its leadership on these issues should be considered. As examples, the complexity of coordinating foreign assistance across the executive branch has only been exacerbated by the crisis. Similarly, in recent months White House staff members in the NSC and NEC have confronted the growing demands of supporting international "summitry" whether it is APEC, the G-20, or the G-8. And hot button economic issues such as outdated export controls have gained prominence as U.S. exports have precipitously slowed. While the previous administration undertook reforms in these and other areas, additional retooling of the international economic policy coordination function deserves serious consideration.

Recommendation 9:   The administration should contemplate significant restructuring and additional resources for the international economic function within the NEC/NSC to, among other things, help rationalize disparate development priorities and organizations; support the expanding "sherpa" support function to advance the U.S. multilateral economic agenda; and ensure needed leadership on critical but complex economic issues like export controls.

Fourth, the speed and interconnectedness of global financial markets and the importance of market developments to economic and political stability around the world argue for a review of the adequacy of current sources of economic and market intelligence. For example, in 2008 the Treasury Department created a "Markets Room" for monitoring daily developments, while the intelligence community focused its efforts and dedicated additional resources to the economic intelligence mission. However, critical questions remain over how to improve the collection of critical economic information, how and to whom it should be provided, what trends should be most carefully monitored over time, and what potential economic "hot spots" pose risks for the future. Inevitably, such assessments will often be more wrong than right, but the process of thinking through such risk factors is a valuable component of a disciplined policy process.

Recommendation 10: The administration should conduct a strategic review and reform, as appropriate, the process for collecting, refining, and distributing economic information and intelligence in the policymaking process.

Finally, the organizational pressures imposed by the financial crisis have revealed the necessity for building greater capabilities and adding additional resources to the international economic arena. As examples, the NEC/NSC international economic staff in the White House, comprised of eight to ten professionals on detail from around the government, or the 150 policy professionals in the International Division at the Treasury are inadequate to deal with the range of complex issues facing the United States. Further, despite excellent experience within government, very few of these professionals have private sector experience or hands-on familiarity with the financial markets. Thus, a key priority is to address the growing need for both career civil servants and political appointees to gain a deeper and more technical understanding of global financial markets.

Recommendation 11: The administration should undertake an economic "talent review" aimed at identifying needed resources, improving the recruiting function and incentive structure to add needed skills and expertise from the private sector, and providing critical training to the outstanding civil servants already in place.

The United States is currently confronting economic challenges that are unprecedented in their breadth and complexity. Economic policymakers must first and foremost ensure the effectiveness of the unprecedented steps already taken to arrest this crisis. But, they must simultaneously confront a broad and diverse range of longer-term economic challenges that will require them to make difficult policy choices and transform existing institutions and processes to maximize the efficacy of their efforts. While U.S. leadership on international economic policy will surely be more difficult in the future than it has been in the past, it is more crucial than ever. The suggestions made here are a first step on the critical and necessary path toward reform.

David McCormick is currently the Distinguished Service Professor of Information Technology, Public Policy and Management at Carnegie Mellon's Heinz College. He is the former Under Secretary for International Affairs within the United States Department of the Treasury. Previously, he served as Deputy National Security Advisor to the President for International Economic Affairs. Prior to that, he served as the Under Secretary of Commerce for Industry and Security. Prior to his government service, Mr. McCormick was President and CEO of FreeMarkets and President of Ariba. He received a Mechanical Engineering degree from the U.S. Military Academy at West Point and a Ph.D. from the Woodrow Wilson School of Public and International Affairs at Princeton University.

[1] U.S. Department of Treasury, Office of Financial Stability, *TARP Allocation Report*, 30 June 2009. The Office of Financial Stability is comprised of new hires as well as individuals on detail from other parts of the government.

[2] Lori Montgomery, "Power of Stimulus Slow to Take Hold," *Washington Post*, 8 July 2009.

[3] U.S. GDP statistics are taken from the Bureau of Economic Analysis at the U.S. Department of Commerce. Global figures are drawn from the World Bank and IMF World Economic Outlook Database.

[4] A number of drivers of U.S. GDP growth in the past—personal consumption enabled by consumer debt, increases in global exports, and expansion of and innovation within the financial services industry—are unlikely to be as strong in the foreseeable future. Also, when the economy turns,

the Federal Reserve will have to act urgently to shrink its balance sheet to ensure price stability, with likely consequences for economic growth. Finally, the recent increase in spending to support government programs places an enormous burden on the U.S. fiscal outlook that can only be addressed in a "slow growth" scenario by raising taxes or reducing spending, or both, with obvious consequences for economic growth.

[5] U.S. Department of Commerce, Bureau of Economic Analysis.

[6] U.S. Department of Commerce, *Visas and Foreign Direct Investment: Supporting U.S. Competitiveness by Facilitating International Travel,* November 2007.

[7] This first idea is drawn from Lael Brainard's paper at the 2008 Aspen Strategy Group, "Can America Still Lead in the Global Economy?"

Part **4**

CONSEQUENCES FOR DEVELOPMENT
AND DEMOCRACY

CHAPTER 8

Priorities for Progress:
Security and Development at a Time of
Global Economic Turmoil

Sylvia Mathews Burwell
President, Global Development Program
Bill & Melinda Gates Foundation

CHAPTER 9

The Impact of the Global Financial Crisis on Democracy

Michael Green
Senior Adviser and Japan Chair
Center for Strategic and International Studies

"Poverty and insecurity are closely related concepts, and their entanglement raises some questions about how policymakers and practitioners should allocate limited resources between them."

— SYLVIA MATHEWS BURWELL

Priorities for Progress:
Security and Development at a Time of Global Economic Turmoil

Sylvia Mathews Burwell[1]
President, Global Development Program
Bill & Melinda Gates Foundation

Historically, discussions of development and foreign aid often open with gloom and despair: starving toddlers, mothers dying in childbirth, women farmers scraping at tiny plots of barren land. Such suffering is real, and demands our response—but our focus should be on solutions and opportunities more than problems and obstacles. Global poverty is not fated. Progress is possible. Many answers are available already. And development success can be a driver of human security.

Indeed, the past two decades reflect real gains in the lives of millions of poor people around the world, in higher incomes, better nutrition, immunization against preventable diseases, and access to education, shelter, clean water, and basic sanitation. We've also seen structural shifts around the world that help bolster the fight against poverty—such as a new generation of technocratic leaders in developing country ministries and central banks, who have tightened the reins on macroeconomic management.

Even in Africa, often viewed as global poverty's Ground Zero, there have been inspiring strides in recent years. Between 2005 and 2007, average real gross domestic product (GDP) was 6.4 percent (excluding South Africa), and twenty-two countries could boast growth rates of 5 percent or higher. There were five democracies on the African continent at the end of the Cold War; there are almost thirty today. We've seen tightly contested elections in Ghana and elsewhere, with peaceful handovers of power between parties. We've seen women taking on greater roles in the social, economic, and political lives of their societies, including the election of Ellen Johnson Sirleaf as Liberia's president, and a greater proportion of female parliamentarians in Rwanda than in any other legislature in the world.

While infectious disease remains a serious threat across the continent, some countries have made significant gains in tackling HIV/AIDS and malaria. And while Africa's private sector still confronts too much red tape, the World Bank's 2009 Doing Business report ranks Senegal, Botswana, and Burkina Faso among the top ten reformers.

As a result, some differentiation among the countries of the continent is starting to occur. Rather than caricaturing Africa as one giant cauldron of dysfunction, global investors, policymakers, and tourists are distinguishing the region's high performers, as they did with the Tigers who pulled out from the pack of Asian poverty after 1960.

A Global Setback

But now, the global economic crisis is putting those gains at risk—and threatening to set back the chances for future development progress as well. The World Bank is predicting a global economic contraction of 3 percent, and the repercussions may be worst for the countries least to blame. As Kofi Annan and members of the Africa Progress Panel have noted, "The tragedy is that when millions of Africans believed their countries and continent were finally on the right track, their hopes are being dashed by problems whose roots lie elsewhere. While the global crisis and climate change are creations of the North, it is Africa which is worst affected and least able to cope."[2]

Private capital flows to developing countries shrank from more than $1 trillion in 2007 to $707 billion in 2008, and are projected to plummet to $363 billion this year. After years of strong growth, remittances to developing countries—more than $300 billion in 2008—are projected to fall by between 5 and 8 percent. Bilateral aid budgets in donor countries are feeling the pinch, and private philanthropic wealth is evaporating; some major foundations have offered buyouts to staff and closed offices overseas.

Funding constraints are also forcing non-governmental development and relief organizations that deliver aid and implement programs on the ground to lay off staff and cut back their operations. While it is too soon to know how deep or prolonged the impact of the financial crisis will be on this community, early data from 2009 do not bode well. A survey of forty-four diverse InterAction members reveals that more than half of the organizations expect to end 2009 with a budget deficit and to have set salary freezes and travel restrictions. More than half of those surveyed have received less or significantly less funding in the first quarter of 2009 compared to the same period last year. More than a third have reduced the size of their staff. For the moment, most of the organizations have not had to reduce their field presence or cut programs, yet nearly a third are seriously considering that option.

Meanwhile, trade is falling off and commodity prices have collapsed, easing prices on imports of food and fuel, but sending shockwaves through export-driven economies. Botswana has had to learn the hard way that diamonds aren't forever: Gem mining operations have been severely cut back, with more than 4,500 jobs lost. South Africa's gold production has shrunk to early 1920s levels. Zambian mines have closed and 8,000 jobs have been lost as copper prices have plunged. As a result, according to World Bank president Robert Zoellick, the overall financing gap for developing countries will be between $350 and $635 billion in 2009, far more than public monies can fill.

In many developing countries, last year's food and fuel crises had already created hardship. Now, because of the economic crisis, tens of millions could lose their jobs, as many as 55 to 90 million more people could be trapped in extreme poverty, and more than a billion could go hungry. These big numbers take their cruelest toll on the smallest members of the human family: Reduced access to food, nutrition, and immunization could translate into an additional 1.4 to 2.8 million infant deaths between now and 2015. Some poor parents are withdrawing their children from school in order to save precious income—and when education is sacrificed, a pathway out of poverty may be closed off forever.

Advanced economies have been using monetary tools and fiscal stimulus to address the downturn. An estimated $2 trillion in fiscal stimulus has been announced so far, with around $900 billion likely to be spent in 2009. But many developing countries cannot cut interest rates without facing the risk of inflation. And though they, too, need fiscal stimulus, the World Bank estimates that only one-quarter of vulnerable developing countries are in a position to provide it. With aid tightening, trade falling, and external financing flows shutting off, many developing countries can neither earn nor borrow the resources needed to boost, or even maintain, spending—putting them at risk of a dangerous downward spiral wherein reduced incomes lead to reduced consumption, which in turn further reduces incomes.

Security Under Threat

These trends have implications for geopolitical and human security in both the short and long term. Even before the financial crisis, poverty killed millions of people every year. Now, as economic instability threatens to undermine law and order, especially in fragile states, American defense experts increasingly view the economic crisis and its geopolitical implications as a critical and pressing security concern. Already last year, there were demonstrations in more than thirty countries that had been hit by rising food and fuel prices.

With regard to Africa, home to the vast majority of the world's least developed countries, the high-level Africa Progress Panel noted in June 2009 that "The economic crisis has now made the poorest of [Africans] even more vulnerable to sudden shocks, reduced the opportunities available to them, and frustrated their hopes. Their frustration could turn latent political divergences into acute strife and political contests into civil wars as parties fight for total power or access to resources."[3]

To be sure, the degree to which poverty causes or contributes to unrest is a matter of debate. But poor economic growth, low income levels, and dependence on natural resources are statistically compelling predictors of civil conflict.

More alarming still is the possibility that a country will be sucked into a vortex in which human desperation helps spark a descent into violence, damaging homes and cropland, poisoning the climate for investment, draining public funding from basic services, and further aggravating the poverty, disease, and degradation that helped trigger the conflict in the first place. At the extreme, failing states can become hothouses of insecurity, spawning cross-border threats from terrorism to trafficking—a disastrous interplay between poverty and insecurity that U.S. Ambassador to the UN Susan Rice has described as a "doom spiral."

But if development assistance can thus be understood as a defensive shield against a world of chaos, there is a proactive, affirmative case for supporting development too: not simply to prevent poor states from imploding and wreaking havoc on their neighbors, but to promote shared advancements in health, education, and opportunity—a rising "success spiral" that points the way to a better, more prosperous, safer world for us all.

Economically, it is in our own best interest to help poor countries unlock their tremendous potential. Most resources for development lie in developing countries themselves, from natural bounty to youthful populations. If we can help developing countries unleash their own assets and nurture the policy and economic environment that will allow the private sector to flourish, the developing world can put itself on the path to lasting prosperity—and in the process, create more sources of creativity, dynamism, and talent, more marketplaces for goods, services, and ideas, and more new partners for global growth, from which we can all benefit. Sustained growth and economic demand in developing countries will help the industrial world recover from the present downturn and expand the playing field where it competes for business. The economic crisis and reduced potential for growth in the developed world increases the need for and importance of realizing more of the developing world's potential for growth. Promoting growth in developing countries is challenging, but it has become even more important to focus on this task.

Indeed, as the Africa Progress Panel noted, developing countries can contribute in a meaningful way to global economic recovery, as more investment in infrastructure, renewable energy, agriculture, and telecommunications creates not only jobs in Africa but also markets for developed and developing countries alike.

Strategically, lending other nations a helping hand in development earns good will that U.S. policymakers can draw on in other areas. As the recent CSIS Commission on Smart Power noted, "Investing in development makes it more likely that governments and citizens will take decisions to stand by America's side when we need allies most."[4] And it is not just recipients of aid who appreciate American generosity. When we help others around the world to realize their aspirations, it shows that our nation stands for something larger than ourselves.

Morally, too, there is a strong case for trying to improve development outcomes in distant lands. As Americans, our founding fathers held as self-evident truth that all men are created equal and endowed with inalienable rights, including to life, liberty, and the pursuit of happiness. Our own values are tarnished when one-fifth of humanity is struggling just to stay alive.

Balancing Priorities: Urgency and Patience

Poverty and insecurity are closely related concepts, and their entanglement raises some questions about how policymakers and practitioners should allocate limited resources between them. We know that in the long run development and security are mutually reinforcing. Clearly there are cases where major investments in conflict-ridden or post-conflict societies are in America's strategic interests—to provide a minimum level of stability, to prevent harmful regional spillovers, and to preclude the likelihood of inequity and despair intensifying or reigniting violence.

But America's interests are also served by promoting broader, deeper development gains in education, health, and economic vitality, and we shouldn't discount the value of these payoffs just because they take longer to realize. On the contrary, these are the outcomes on which a stable common future depends— the foundational support for durable growth within communities, countries, and regions. The U.S. government supports this rhetorically, but our spending tells a different story: 38 percent of U.S. foreign assistance spending is devoted to six countries—all of them allies in the war on terror or the war on drugs—and in 2007, nearly one in four U.S. aid dollars went to Iraq or Afghanistan alone.[5]

The United States will never reap the broad stability gains we seek unless we invest more in building the middle—in tending not only to frontline states or to states that are falling apart, but in making sure that stable, poor countries that are on the road to economic growth can stay on that road. Our policymakers should be more proactive and less reactive. They must do more than help poor countries cope with the consequences of economic failure and instability; they must take advantage of opportunities to help stable countries that are doing well sustain and reinforce their progress. If development and security are to move forward hand in hand, we need to take a long-term view, investing not only in crisis management but in crisis prevention; patient support for core development in poor states moving in the right direction.

The Bill & Melinda Gates Foundation Approach

At the Bill & Melinda Gates Foundation, we believe we can have the greatest impact in turning the tide on global poverty by focusing on effective, scalable, and sustainable solutions to problems that affect the lives of millions of people and have the potential for significant breakthroughs. When development solutions are scalable and sustainable, they contribute to security, too.

We know, for example, that three-quarters of all people subsisting on less than $1 a day live in rural areas, and most rely on agriculture for their food and income. We also know that when agricultural development takes off, the payoff for human development can be enormous. The Green Revolution, for example, doubled the amount of food produced, reduced food prices for the poor, saved hundreds of millions of lives, and laid the groundwork for broader development in many countries. More recently, in Ghana, strong agricultural growth has helped drive an overall GDP growth of 4.8 percent over the past fifteen years—allowing it to nearly halve the poverty rate since 1990.

And yet, both donors and developing countries have severely underinvested in agriculture. The percentage of official development assistance that went to agriculture fell from more than 16 percent in 1980 to less than 4 percent in 2004. During that same period, absolute assistance fell from nearly $7 billion to less than $3.5 billion. And, adjusted for inflation, the World Bank cut its agricultural lending from $7.7 billion to $2 billion—even as, from 1980 to 2006, the United States cut its support for agricultural development by nearly three-quarters, from $2.3 billion to $624 million.

The foundation has committed more than $1.4 billion to date to revitalize agricultural development, with a focus on small farmers. Through programs such as AGRA (the Alliance for a Green Revolution in Africa), we are working with partners to invest across the agricultural value chain—from seeds and soil to farm management and market access—so that millions of small farmers, most of whom are women, have the tools and opportunities to lift themselves out of hunger and poverty for good and to pass the benefits on to their children in the form of health care, schooling, and hope.

Similarly, we believe financial services can be transformative for the world's poor, so we're funding innovations in technological design and delivery that lower the costs and increase the value of delivering financial services to the poor, quickly, broadly, and sustainably. We believe it is possible—within a single generation—for billions of poor people in the developing world to gain access to affordable, safe savings accounts that help create financial security, allowing people to securely set aside small sums of money so they can pay for a health crisis or invest in an opportunity like schooling for their children or buying a sewing machine to start a business.

The Way Ahead

Philanthropic investments like the ones described above have long-term horizons, but they affect people immediately and directly, providing stability for the individuals and families who are the bedrock of stable communities. We believe this patient, long-term approach remains the right one, even in a time of economic turmoil. The current crisis has not altered the recipe for achieving development success. What it has changed—for private and governmental donors alike—is the urgency and emphasis we must place on operational implementation.

There are three key areas that demand special focus: money, effectiveness, and leadership.

Money

The developed world must keep its promises on development assistance to prevent the financial crisis from derailing years of hard-fought development gains. In a time of tight money, it is hard but essential for governments to stick to their funding pledges and for advocates to help build awareness and support among publics understandably preoccupied with their own economic concerns.

It is tempting to focus development funds and staff time on strategic countries in crisis like Pakistan and Afghanistan, but policymakers must grasp that there are different types of development challenges—and different ways of viewing our strategic priorities—that require different types of responses from government. Inevitably, attention and resources tend to focus on countries where there are compelling national security interests at stake. To be sure, development is an important part of the wider nation-building effort in Afghanistan and Pakistan, and there is good reason to invest in development projects that can, over the long term, help build and maintain security, which is a necessary condition for political stability and economic progress. While that is a good rationale for development in these cases, it is not the best rationale for investing in development more broadly. It is not even the best national security rationale for investing in development.

Instead, the U.S. government ought to view development as a long-term effort to foster widespread and lasting "success spirals" that will reduce security risks over the long term, build up new markets, and expand local, regional, and international economic opportunities. As international donors increase funding for important development work in unstable states, they should take care not to crowd out investment in stable countries like Mozambique and Ghana, where there are opportunities to foster success and reinforce wider regional stability over the long term. If we focus too much on building security in unstable, strategic countries as a rationale for development—and if this is the main arena in which our development staff focus their attention and budgets—in the future we may find ourselves, again, working in difficult and dangerous situations that might have been avoided with a smarter, more farsighted strategy.

In practice, U.S. foreign policy needs to consider core development investments in more stable developing countries as a critical strategic priority along with the important development needs in Afghanistan and Pakistan. Countries like Mozambique, Tanzania, and Ghana that have recently combined peaceful democratic transfers of power with strong economic growth (beginning from a very low base) need and deserve long-term support that can reinforce these trends and help provide wider regional stability over the long term. The Millennium Challenge Corporation (MCC), for which the last Bush administration deserves credit, is a good example of how government can recognize and act on core development priorities and reward well-performing poor countries doing the right thing. While it has taken more time than it should have to get the MCC effectively up and running, it is now working relatively well and is a model worth supporting, even if it takes time to get right.

The Obama administration's announcement that it would request an additional $1 billion investment in development assistance for food security in 2010—explicitly excluding assistance to Afghanistan and Pakistan, to be dealt with in separate requests—is another good example of how government can distinguish core or long-term development priorities from a category of national security interests that are intertwined with, but different from, core development. This approach has already paid dividends by helping leverage additional international resources for a new Group of 8-sponsored $20 billion food security initiative over the next three years. The simple fact is that we will do a better job planning for both defense and development if we can make this distinction more often and more clearly. One practical way to do this would be to explain what counts (and why) as core or long-term development in the foreign assistance budget so that we can assess aid allocation decisions at the policy level and define plans and objectives for different categories of assistance that are essentially designed for different purposes.

In the immediate future, as project funding channeled through non-governmental implementing agencies shrinks, particularly in the United States, NGOs must strive to become as efficient and effective as possible. To do more with less, NGOs and donors need to help one another channel resources towards concepts that we know can work. This will require building a new kind of trust: Implementers need to tell donors the unvarnished truth about their efforts and results; donors must distinguish between successful implementation (running projects and generating outputs) and impact (whether or not projects, however well implemented, work), and factor this distinction into their funding decisions. In a results-based development world, we must recognize that when things go wrong, it may not be a failure of the NGO, but rather a failure of the project concept. Unfortunately, building this trust will probably take time—but we need to make this shift in donor-implementer relations, and now is a good time to start. Also, and importantly, we should not forget that even as donors work with NGO project implementers, there are other ways to deliver aid effectively, including through budget support to responsible governments.

In addition, the industrialized world must support multilateral institutions like the World Bank and the International Monetary Fund in devising ways to help poor countries bridge the credit gap, such as funding the World Bank's Vulnerability Finance Facility and boosting the IMF's concessional lending capacity. Earlier this spring, with the support of the World Bank and other partners, Liberia's commercial creditors agreed to buy back $1.2 billion of debt at a 97 percent discount. Such measures are important but insufficient. Relieved of its debts, Liberia will find it easier—but not easy—to move forward with its development programs.

This work must be done at the retail level, differentiated and diligent, putting together the deals that meet each country's specific needs. It will require expert leadership from the IMF and World Bank, engagement from the United Nations and funding support from member states, recognizing there are no one-size-fits-all solutions to the varied hardships the crisis has created in developing countries around the world.

The recent financial crisis underscores the notion that fostering stable, widespread economic growth in the developing world is important for the global economy. When we think of development, we ought to think more often about the value of emerging markets and what we can do to help poor countries become stronger sources of global demand for goods and services. Beginning now, industrial countries should open more and stronger trade links with poor countries, including expanding their "aid for trade" projects and dismantling trade barriers that discriminate against developing countries, especially in agriculture. Coming out of the current recession, developed countries will benefit from greater trade with and within the developing world. Rising demand from households and businesses in Asia, Latin America, and Africa could help prop up the global economy when industrial economies are weak. And over the longer term, more and stronger emerging markets will generate more business opportunities around the world. Although economic growth does pose some challenges that will need to be addressed in wider forums—for instance by potentially driving up energy prices and greenhouse gas emissions—that growth should temper future economic downturns and perhaps even help to reduce the time it takes for the world economy to recover from the current crisis.

Developing countries, too, must uphold their commitment to fund advances in their people's well-being. Through the Comprehensive Africa Agriculture Development Programme, for example, African governments agreed in 2003 to devote 10 percent of their national budgets to agriculture to help raise agricultural productivity by at least 6 percent by 2015. Countries such as Ethiopia, Madagascar, Mali, and Niger have surpassed the 10 percent target, but will be hard-pressed to sustain spending levels in the face of the financial crisis. They should maintain their commitment to agriculture and other nations should follow their lead.

Effectiveness

Yet discussions of development assistance are only meaningful if aid is made more effective. This was true before the economic crisis struck, and it is even more relevant now.

What would it take to drive a transformation in U.S. aid effectiveness? First, the United States needs a comprehensive national development strategy. Such a strategy would tackle up-front the difficult questions inherent in setting priorities: What does success look like? How do we think about the range of development needs in conflict, post-conflict, and stable but extremely poor states? How do we balance short- and long-term goals? What does the United States government do best, and where should other development actors take the lead? Clarifying our own strategy will enable the United States to impose more coherence and coordination among our development assistance efforts, a crucial first step in improving aid effectiveness.

Second, we need to do a better job of thinking of poor people not just as aid beneficiaries, but as our clients and partners. In part, that means supporting developing country leaders as they devise economic plans for long-term growth and self-sufficiency. But it also means having the humility, as donors, to put aside our own views of what should be done and preconceptions of how to do it, and to be more attentive to our assistance partners' needs and norms.

To give an example, agricultural scientists have developed cowpea varieties that poor farmers can store for longer periods of time, preventing spoilage from robbing them of precious food and income. Yet African farmers, the majority of whom are women, have resisted adopting modified cowpeas. Why? Because these new cowpeas tend to be very hard and take longer to cook, which is a burden that women alone have to bear. Had the women's priorities been better understood from the start, the development outcome might have been better, too. Based on what we're learning from experiences like this one, the Bill & Melinda Gates Foundation has started a process of mainstreaming gender in our existing agriculture grants so that gender becomes part of the planning process, not the cause of unintended consequences.

Third, donors need to do a better job of coordinating their efforts. Between 1993 and 2005, the number of donor aid projects initiated each year nearly tripled from 10,000 to 28,000, a proliferation of programs that likely included duplication, while adding to the administrative demands on strapped recipient country bureaucracies. Some donor countries have generated even more confusion by dividing responsibility for development assistance among multiple agencies; the United States, for example, has over fifty different federal agencies responsible for 150 policy directives and goals.

Finally, the United States will be most effective in delivering against the strategy and philosophy above if it focuses on bolstering the operational ability to achieve success. That includes changing Office of Personnel Management hiring rules to get the right people in place. It means giving public servants at State and USAID the right training, from day one, with the same kind of rigor and sense of mission we provide our men and women in uniform. It means assuring the right career incentives for Foreign Service professionals, such that all aspiring ambassadors know they have to be fluent in development strategy, goals, and challenges, and be able to show success in promoting development results on the ground.

It also means the administration must work with Congress to fund State and USAID appropriately. As a bipartisan group of eight former secretaries of state recently argued, more than a quarter of State Department posts requiring foreign language proficiency are filled by Foreign Service officers who lack those skills, and there are fewer career officers at USAID today than there once were in Vietnam alone. President Obama has taken a good first step with his 2010 budget request, including funding for more than 1,200 new positions at State and $1.7 billion "to strengthen USAID's operational capacity, putting the Agency on a path to double its overseas Foreign Service officer workforce by 2012."[6] Still, more must to be done to bring these agencies to their full potential.

The United States should also maximize existing U.S. development efforts such as PEPFAR (the President's Emergency Plan for AIDS Relief), the Millennium

Challenge Corporation, and the aid being delivered by the Department of Defense, beginning with a clearer articulation of how each agency contributes to success in the overarching development strategy.

Leadership

A final element for development success is strong, capable, and determined leadership, which donors and recipients alike agree is the only way developing countries can move up the ladder to aid independence. Leadership is important under any circumstances, of course, but it becomes all the more crucial in times of crisis, when the stakes are high and lives are on the line.

Developing countries themselves must produce accountable, effective government officials, but it is in America's clear interest to support them as they do—and this is the case whether we're talking about Pakistan, Honduras, or any other nation in the world. Beyond financial assistance, support can include offering public recognition to leaders who stay on the hard road to reform, as Sudanese business executive and philanthropist Mo Ibrahim has done with his Index of African Governance and his Prize for Achievement in African Leadership. The United States should also help developing country leaders build strong teams of public servants around them and invest in the civil society organizations that will hold state officials accountable—as the Open Society Institute has done in Liberia, for example, through grants to the Governance Reform Commission to help the Liberian state renew itself and to a host of civic organizations in areas from human rights to the legal system to the press.

Yet developing countries are not the only places where leadership matters. The United States, too, must build a cadre of development experts and champions who can raise development's profile on the foreign policy agenda.

That begins with truly valuing development's contribution to America's national security goals, and clarifying the qualifications we seek in our development leaders—such as experience in the field, experience in government, and experience in the private sector to hone the diplomatic, political, and results-oriented skills essential for development success.

It also demands that we elevate the concept of "smart power" and "smart aid" in the national security conversation and bring development experts from the margins into the mainstream of the U.S. foreign policy elite. The emphasis top officials now place on "defense, diplomacy, and development" as the "3 D's" of U.S. foreign policy, and the willingness of influential organizations like the Aspen Strategy Group to incorporate development concerns into its deliberations, are examples of how that shift can take place.

But we're not there yet. How many top university graduates actively aspire to work at USAID or the World Bank, or dream of heading up UNICEF or UNDP? When the development career path holds the same prestige as the private sector or better-known avenues of public service, then we will know the third "D" of U.S. foreign policy has well and truly arrived.

Sylvia Mathews Burwell, President of the Bill & Melinda Gates Foundation, Global Development Program, oversees the foundation's efforts to help the world's poorest people overcome hunger and poverty. She leads Global Development's major areas of grant making: Financial Services for the Poor, Agricultural Development, and Special Initiatives. She also oversees policy and advocacy activities for the Global Development program. She joined the foundation in 2001 as Executive Vice President and served as COO and Executive Director from 2002 to April 2006. Prior to joining the foundation, Mrs. Burwell served in the Clinton Administration as Deputy Director of the Office of Management and Budget, Assistant to the President, Deputy Chief of Staff to the President, and Chief of Staff to former Treasury Secretary Robert E. Rubin. Before joining the federal government, Mrs. Burwell worked for McKinsey and Company, a management consulting firm, where she focused on consulting for financial institutions. Mrs. Burwell serves on the board of directors for MetLife Inc. and the Council on Foreign Relations and is a member of the board of the Alliance for a Green Revolution in Africa. She is a member of the Trilateral Commission and the Nike Foundation Advisory Group. She is a graduate of Harvard University and is a Rhodes Scholar. She is a member of the Aspen Strategy Group.

[1] The views expressed in this paper are the author's own and do not necessarily reflect the views of the Bill & Melinda Gates Foundation.

[2] Graca Machel Annan and Michel Camdessus, "The Future of the State of Africa," The Huffington Post, 10 June 2009, available at http://www.huffingtonpost.com/kofi-annan/the-future-of-the-state-o_b_213710.html.

[3] "An Agenda for Progress at a Time of Global Crisis: A Call for African Leadership," Annual Report of the Africa Progress Panel, 2009. Available at http://africaprogresspanel.socialmediarelease.co.za/files/africanprogresspanel/pdf/APP-ANNUALREPORT-EXEC-SUM-ENGLISH.doc.

[4] Richard L. Armitage, Jr. and Joseph S. Nye, "CSIS Commission on Smart Power: A Smarter, More Secure America," Center for Strategic and International Studies. Available at http://csis.org/files/media/csis/pubs/071106_csissmartpowerreport.pdf.

[5] OECD Development Assistance Committee Database, Table 2a, available at: http://www.oecd.org/document/33/0,2340,en_2649_34447_36661793_1_1_1_1,00.html

[6] Office of Management and Budget, *Budget of the United States Government for Fiscal Year 2010.* Washington: Government Printing Office, 2009.

"The bottom line is that the evidence for a direct endogenous causal relationship between economic development and democratization is debatable. However, economic development is an undeniable complement to democratization."

— MICHAEL J. GREEN

The Impact of the Global Financial Crisis on Democracy

Michael J. Green[1]
Senior Adviser and Japan Chair
Center for Strategic and International Studies

Introduction

The increasing acceptance of democratic norms such as good governance and respect for human rights over the last fifty years has underpinned the neoliberal order and hegemonic stability even as relative U.S. power has declined in the international system. A reversal of these democratic norms globally would accelerate relative U.S. decline and destabilize the system more generally. Does the current financial crisis have the potential to cause such damage?

While economists may be able to model the possible impact of the current financial crisis on exports, employment numbers, or market valuations, it is far more difficult to assess the impact on democratic norms and governance. To begin with, we do not know whether we are at the end or the beginning of the crisis. In addition, there is no theoretical consensus about the causal relationship between economic performance and democratic governance within states. We can point to some historical examples of democracies failing after economic crises, but these precedents are not necessarily generalizable and there are counter examples of economic crises actually accelerating democratization. Nevertheless, it is important that we attempt to understand the knock-on effects of a prolonged economic contraction on the neoliberal order in terms of democratic governance and norms, and not just the more commonly studied pillars of economics and security.

This chapter will posit a framework for anticipating the potential fallout from the financial crisis in terms of democratic norms and governance by drawing from previous work in two areas: First, the large and heavily debated body of social science literature on the correlation and causality between economic performance and democratization; and second, the historical precedents, including Weimar Germany and Taisho Japan during the Great Depression, the Latin American debt crisis in the 1980s, the 1997-1998 Asian financial crisis, and the 1998 Russian default. Using these theoretical and historical discussions as background, the paper will suggest a categorization, or "watch list," of states where democratic norms or governance may be most at risk from the financial crisis. The paper will then examine the question of whether the financial crisis might lead to a broader legitimacy crisis for neoliberal norms, particularly in the face of authoritarian development models like China. The chapter will conclude with a recommendation to re-energize governance and democracy strategies in U.S. foreign policy in anticipation of these possible challenges.

Economic Performance and Democratic Governance

While there is a statistically significant correlation between wealth and democracy (with the outliers being the rich, authoritarian, oil-producing nations of the Middle East at one end and relatively poor democracies like India and Indonesia at the other end), there is no consensus among scholars about whether wealth accumulation in fact leads to democratization. The seminal contemporary work on the subject was Seymour Martin Lipset's "Some Social Requisites of Democracy" in the *American Political Science Review* in 1959.[2] Lipset identified economic development, measured primarily by indices of wealth, as one of the key requisites for democratization, together with other factors such as literacy and urbanization. His work focused on statistical correlation, which left a theoretical gap that sparked a fifty year quest to find the causal link between wealth and freedom.[3]

Subsequent efforts to design tests that would demonstrate the statistical link between wealth and democratization have been mixed. Though there is considerable discussion on exactly how wealth leads to democracy, the role the free market plays in advancing democracy has been debated by Michael Mandelbaum, Francis Fukuyama, and others. There are generally two camps in this debate: those who believe that wealth stimulates democracy and can in fact spark democracy in places where there is none, and those who believe that wealth and democracy are simultaneously caused by wider changes in society. Mandelbaum, for example, falls in the first camp and asserts a fairly direct line from the free market to democracy; he has argued that capitalist systems breed more robust civil societies, with trade and professional organizations, clubs, and other refuges from the state ultimately providing a counterweight to centralized authority. He also contends that capitalism hones the skills necessary for citizens to succeed in a democratic society.[4] This argument was echoed by Ronald Inglehart and Christian Welzel in *Foreign Affairs* in 2009, when they argued that prevailing global trends away from centralization and bureaucratization have led to a cultural shift towards greater individuality, reinforcing democratization.[5]

Other social scientists have rejected efforts at demonstrating direct causality between wealth and democracy. James Robinson argued in the *Annual Review of Political Science* in 2006, for example, that relying on empirical cases without theorizing the causal mechanisms leads scholars to ignore the broader social context necessary for democracy.[6]   He posits a model that emphasizes social factors necessary for democratization; factors that can be impacted by economic development but do not depend upon it.   Evelyn Humber, Dietrich Rueschmeyer, and John Stephens also find that changes in class structure—specifically the creation of a middle class— lead to both wealth and democracy, and that the causal line is therefore not directly from wealth to democracy.[7] Fukuyama has taken a more holistic approach, linking economic growth, civil society, state-building, rule of law, and electoral democracy as "dimensions of development" rather than "requisites."[8]   He acknowledges the importance of "sequencing" between these different elements; for example, it would be illogical to have electoral democracy or rule of law before state-building.

The bottom line is that the evidence for a direct endogenous causal relationship between economic development and democratization is debatable.   However, economic development is an undeniable complement to democratization.[9] Would economic reversals therefore correlate with failures of democracy?

In 1997, Adam Przeworski and Fernando Limongi broke new ground in the democracy-wealth debate by modeling historical examples to demonstrate that the important correlation is not between development and democracy *per se*, but more specifically between development and the sustainability of democratic forms of government once established—what has been termed the "exogenous" effect of development on democracy.[10]   In their examination of why democracies fail, Ethan Kapstein and Nathan Converse found that of the 123 new democracies born between 1964 and 2004, 67 remained democracies and 56 reversed to authoritarianism.[11] In the sustained democracies, the average per capita GDP was $2,618 (in 2006 dollars), while in the failed democracies, the average per capita GDP was $866. Kapstein and Converse noted important exceptions, such as Thailand, where coups have taken place despite economic growth; Russia and Venezuela, where authoritarianism has been reinforced by the increased price of oil; and Eastern Europe, where democracy took root despite relative poverty. They also found that other factors correlated more closely than economic performance (for example, countries with strong executive systems reverted to authoritarianism 70 percent of the time, compared with a 40 percent reversal rate for states with weaker executive systems). But they concluded that economic development and wealth were indeed critical exogenous factors in explaining why some new democracies failed and others did not.

The long (and unfinished) debate about the link between wealth and freedom therefore leads to at least one fairly safe conclusion—that per capita GDP is closely correlated to how well new democracies sustain their liberal form of government. It should follow, then, that decreases in wealth should make new democracies more vulnerable. But on that question of causality and triggering mechanisms, the theory comes up short.

The Historical Precedents

While social scientists have not developed a broadly accepted theory of causality between economic crises and reversals of democracy, history provides examples of what can happen. The most striking cases are Taisho Japan and Weimar Germany during what Samuel Huntington has called the first "reverse wave of democratization" in the 1930s.[12]

Japan by the mid-1920s had developed a vibrant two-party system and great expectations for continued growth and social development based on convergence with the global economy. In 1930, Japan returned to the gold standard (suspended during World War I) only to see Great Britain abandon the standard the next year and the United States pass the Smoot-Hawley tariffs the year after that. The result was massive economic displacement at home as rice and silk prices collapsed, followed by a backlash against economic convergence that led to increased support for the army's agenda of "renovationism," protectionism, and autarky. The civilian political parties quickly fell under the control of the army, following the assassinations of civilian leaders and huge increases in military spending throughout the rest of the 1930s. As Hugh Patrick notes, "slower growth caused, or at least exacerbated, the stresses of industrialization, and the social and political conditions which put the militarists in power."[13] Or, as Jack Snyder puts it more directly, "depression and protectionism helped kill Taisho democracy."[14]

Because of Germany's defeat in the First World War, the Weimar Republic faced far greater structural weaknesses than Japan's Minseito government, including massive reparations, hyper-inflation, and the delegitimizing effects of association with the Versailles treaty. That being said, Germany began recovering after 1923 and by 1929 the standard of living was higher than it had ever been in German history. However, this recovery only papered over the underlying institutional, social, and industrial vulnerabilities of the nation. As the historian A.J.P. Taylor argued in 1946, "the collapse of the republic was accelerated, but not caused, by the economic crisis which swept the entire world between 1929 and 1933...with few supporters and no roots, it fell at the first rumble of thunder."[15] Japan and Germany were different in many respects in the interwar years, but the lesson they share is that new democracies with weak institutional roots and heavy dependence on the international economy can quickly be toppled by international financial contagions.

The post-war examples of financial crises vary in terms of the impact on democratic norms and governance. The Latin American debt crisis in the 1980s had its roots in the import substitution policies of many countries in the region and borrowing that amounted to $29 billion by 1970.[16] With the combination of oil shocks and then U.S. increases in interest rates in the late 1970s, Third World debtors suddenly faced another four or five billion dollars a year in additional interest payments.[17] The financial crisis broke in 1982, when Mexico announced it had run out of money and could not pay its debts. The impact was particularly devastating for authoritarian regimes in the region. In Argentina, inflation hit 400 percent in 1983 and external debt increased to $46 billion. As a result, the economic crisis combined with defeat in the Falklands War to bring down the Galtieri government and usher in a new era of democratically elected leadership.[18] Brazil's more managed return to democratic rule from two decades of military dictatorship was also accelerated when the region's financial crisis helped the opposition defeat the military-backed government in elections in 1985. On the other hand, the collapse of oil prices in the 1980s led to instability in Venezuela and eventually to the 1992 coup attempts and the election of Hugo Chavez as president, reversing steps the country had taken towards democratization.[19] (Though this leads to a separate discussion of the impact of petrodollars and the price of oil on authoritarian, oil-rich nations and does not link directly to the financial crisis in Latin America.) Overall, the region saw a general trend towards democratization that was prompted at least in part by the debt crisis in the 1980s.

The impact of the 1997-1998 East Asia financial crisis on democracy in the region was more pronounced than in Latin America because many of Asia's authoritarian governments relied more heavily on economic performance for legitimacy and because the crisis had its roots in the nature of the affected countries' political economies. The crisis was caused primarily by inadequate financial sector supervision, poor assessment and management of financial risk, and maintenance of relatively fixed exchange rates that prompted heavy international borrowing, much of it short-term and denominated in foreign currency.[20]   In 1998, the Indonesian economy contracted by more than 13 percent[21] and the poverty rate more than doubled from 15 percent in 1997 to 33 percent in 1998.[22]   Suharto resigned in May of that year and after two parliamentary-elected governments, Indonesians were able to go to the polls in 2004 and 2009 to elect the president directly. While South Koreans had already elected their presidents in open elections in 1988 and 1992, the 1997-1998 financial crisis played a role in breaking the conservatives' dominance of the political process by demonstrating the moral hazard inherent in the cozy ties between the business *chaebol* and the ruling politicians. Kim Dae Jung's victory in the December 1997 election opened up a more competitive electoral process between conservatives and progressives and strengthened Korea's overall record on governance and Koreans' strong identity with democratic norms.[23]

Russia's economy was also severely impacted by the Asian contagion in 1998, as speculation against the ruble triggered a renewed spike in interest rates to 50 percent and Russia defaulted on its debt payments in August of that year, despite an International Monetary Fund (IMF) and World Bank rescue package of $22.6 billion. While there are many factors that led to Boris Yeltsin's resignation on New Year's Eve 1999 and his successor Vladimir Putin's return to authoritarianism, the 1998 ruble crisis was clearly one of the triggers. In that sense, the Russian return to authoritarianism perhaps bears more resemblance to the democratic reversals in Weimar Germany and Taisho Japan than to the contemporaneous examples in Indonesia or Korea, where the financial crisis undermined the legitimacy of decades-old cronyism rather than highlighting new cronyism that accompanied democratization.

Resilient and Threatened Democracies

In summary, there is a broad consensus on the general correlation between economic performance and democratization, but not on the triggers or causality. History does demonstrate some financial crisis triggering mechanisms that lead to reversals of democracies, but also highlights the fact that financial crisis can undermine authoritarian states and prompt democratization. In both theory and history, there appear to be three variables that determine the ultimate impact of a financial crisis on democratic norms and governance: 1) the degree of exposure to international financial markets; 2) the resilience of democratic institutions (making newer democracies in transition more vulnerable); and 3) the degree to which the political system (as opposed to political parties) draws legitimacy from economic performance.

Given these variables, it is possible to categorize states into six broad categories in terms of the potential impact of the current financial crisis.

1. *Economically exposed, with resilient democratic institutions and less dependence on economic performance for legitimacy of the political system.* This category would essentially cover the member states of the Organization for Economic Cooperation and Development (OECD), where political parties (especially in exporting Asian countries like Japan, Korea, and Taiwan) are at risk, but democratic governance and institutions are not.

2. *Economically exposed, with less resilient (or newer) democratic institutions and dependence on economic performance for legitimacy of the political system.* This category would include the Baltic states (for example, Latvia, which suffered a 12.9 percent economic contraction and 15.4 percent inflation in 2008 and saw the government fall), Central Europe (for example, Hungary, which was forced to take an IMF bailout), and Eastern Europe (for example, Romania, which Goldman Sachs rated the second most vulnerable economy in Eastern Europe in 2009). Across Eastern and Central Europe right wing/anti-immigrant and anti-Semitic politicians scored well in recent European parliamentary elections in the wake of the crisis, demonstrating the pernicious effect of the financial crisis on democratic institutions and civil society. However, the legitimacy of democratic norms in these countries is also undergirded by the European Union and European integration.

   In Southeast Asia, this category might also include Thailand and the Philippines, although their economies have declined by less than the European countries mentioned above,[24] making them less vulnerable. Latin American states with less than three decades since democratization may fall into this category as well.

3. *Economically less exposed, with new democratic institutions and system legitimacy contingent on economic performance.* This category might include Indonesia, where the impact of the current economic crisis has been muted because

of Indonesia's relatively insulated banking system and low dependency on exports for growth (20 percent of GDP, compared with 70 percent for Thailand).

4. *Authoritarian systems, exposed to the international economy, with heavy dependence on economic performance for legitimacy.* This category would include China and Vietnam, where further displacement could change governance and democratic norms in a positive direction (reminiscent of Indonesia after the 1997 financial crisis) or in a more repressive direction (reminiscent of Russia in 1998 or even Taisho Japan).[25] Russia may also fit in this category, though the Kremlin may rely less on economic performance for legitimacy of the system than does China or Vietnam.

5. *Authoritarian systems, not exposed to the international economy and not dependent on economic growth for legitimacy.* This category would include states like North Korea, Burma, and Cuba (acknowledging that each is more reliant on external economic investment or assistance than the regimes acknowledge). While it seems unlikely that a prolonged financial crisis would precipitate regime change or democratization in these states, the resulting entropy in the system and tension among major actors might give greater leeway for destabilizing external actions or increased internal repression by these states.

6. *Weak states, exposed to the international economy and vulnerable to the impact of increased poverty.* The World Bank has estimated that 53 million people living in emerging markets will fall back into absolute poverty this year.[26] This category would include much of sub-Saharan Africa, where foreign reserves in countries like the Democratic Republic of the Congo and the Central African Republic have dwindled and governments are approaching the point where they will not be able to import essentials. (In 2007, African countries raised $6.5 billion selling bonds on international markets, this year the amount was zero, exacerbating a crisis prompted by the collapse in commodity prices.)[27]

This presents a first cut at placing countries within these six categories in terms of potential changes in democracy and governance resulting from a prolonged financial crisis. There are obviously important actors in the system that do not fit neatly in any of the six. India, for example, could be placed in category three with Indonesia, since India has been relatively insulated from the impact of the crisis. (India relies on exports for only about 21 percent of GDP (2007)[28] and on foreign direct investment (FDI) for only 0.82 percent of GDP (2005),[29] suggesting internal demand and a relatively lower exposure to the effects of a sustained financial crisis than more export or FDI dependent neighboring economies.) However, India's democratic form of government is now sixty years old, putting it closer to category one democracies like the United States or Japan. On the other hand, India shares many of the governance challenges (like corruption) and the potential for sectarian violence that lie just beneath the surface with Indonesia. Another difficult case would be Iran, which shares many attributes with category five states like North Korea and Burma, but also is trending towards Vietnam or China in terms of economic exposure and the relative importance of economic performance for regime legitimacy.[30] Iran's dependence on exports for GDP growth has been steadily growing, from 14.4 percent in 1990 to 22.7 percent in 2000 and 28.3 percent in 2008; not quite a Thailand or Vietnam (with 70 percent of GDP dependent on exports in 2008), but not that far from China, with 40 percent. The increase in unemployment in Iran from 10.5 percent in 2005 to estimates of 17 percent in 2008 may also have played a role in the recent demonstrations against the regime. We may find in retrospect that the financial crisis played a role in changing Iran the way it did Indonesia in 1998, but it is far to soon to know.

Of the six categories listed above, the states most susceptible to damage from the economic crisis in terms of democratic norms and governance would be in category two (economically exposed, with less resilient or newer democratic institutions and dependence on economic performance for legitimacy of the political system). However, many of these newer democracies do have the ability to increase their resistance to the effects of the crisis in Europe because they are embedded in the European Union. In East Asia, the Association of Southeast Asian Nations (ASEAN) and other regional organizations do not yet play the same supporting role, but major regional democracies such as Japan, Korea, or Indonesia could play a greater role providing support for democratic institutions. U.S. democracy support in both cases should be built around multilateral and regional approaches.

Category four states (authoritarian systems, exposed to the international economy, with heavy dependence on economic performance for legitimacy) would be of significant concern in terms of potential impact on the international system, but our tools to strengthen good governance or civil society in these states are more limited because of the authoritarian nature of their governments. Nevertheless, because history suggests that this category has enormous potential for change (in either positive or negative directions), the United States and other democracies should seek collaborative ways to work with these governments to strengthen the accountability of domestic institutions and the durability of civil society.

Category five states (authoritarian systems, not exposed to the international economy and not dependent on economic growth for legitimacy) present the hardest nuts to crack. However, it is precisely because of the potential that these states will increase repression at times of international distraction that the United States has a particular responsibility to focus international attention on the human rights situations in these countries.

Category six (weak states, exposed to the international economy and vulnerable to the impact of increased poverty) presents in many respects a more immediate humanitarian than governance problem, though ultimately improved governance is critical to pulling these states out of their longer-term humanitarian crises.

Economic Performance and the Legitimacy of Democratic Norms

In addition to the impact of the financial crisis on democratic norms and governance within states, there is the potential that the current financial crisis could destroy the legitimacy of democratic norms across the international system. Even before the onset of the current crisis, a debate was brewing about whether China's model of authoritarian development was a challenge to the prevailing neoliberal norms because Beijing was successfully growing without liberalizing.[31]   A number of authors have argued that the gravitational pull of China's economy and Beijing's new soft power are already succeeding in supplanting neoliberal norms in parts of East Asia and Africa.[32]   Since the financial crisis broke, Roger Altman and others have argued that China will only increase its normative challenge to the neoliberal order, since Beijing is poised to emerge from the economic crisis in stronger shape than the United States, Japan, or the EU.[33]

The ideational balance of power (the relative influence of neoliberal norms vis-à-vis the neo-authoritarian norms of China or Russia) is an important element in the global balance of power as China's power rises relative to the United States. But does China represent an attractive new model of political governance? In 2008, the Chicago Council on Global Affairs conducted public opinion surveys in the United States, China, Japan, South Korea, Vietnam, and Indonesia on how each of these six nations perceived the attractiveness and influence of their own and their neighbors' diplomatic, cultural, economic, and social soft power. Across the region, the United States was ranked highest, followed by Japan and then China. (The major outliers were Americans, who saw their influence in the region as weaker than the region saw it, and Chinese, who saw their influence as greater than the region actually saw it.)[34]

The Asian Barometer survey taken in 2006-2007 found that East Asians listed "democratic" forms of government as the most preferred regime type by a large margin.[35] And a 2008 survey of elites conducted by the Center for Strategic and International studies in nine Asian countries found that after "confidence building," "preventing interstate conflict," and "economic cooperation," the next four goals listed across the region as essential for East Asian community building over the coming decade were "good governance," "human rights," "free and fair elections," and "strengthening domestic political institutions."[36] While these four norms ranked relatively lower in China than in the rest of the region, they nevertheless were cited by more than 50 percent of Chinese respondents as important goals, raising the question of whether there is even a consensus in Beijing about the so-called "Beijing consensus." Indeed, there is evidence of considerable debate within China about whether China's own development path should be sustained, given widening income gaps, regional disparities, corruption, and environmental degradation.[37]

It should also be noted that democracies around China's periphery are increasingly emphasizing their democratic brand in an effort to enhance their own power and legitimacy relative to Beijing's. Japan's former prime minister, Aso Taro, has championed the promotion of an "arc of freedom and prosperity" that has been met with some skepticism in the United States. But behind his somewhat grandiose vision is a consistent and pragmatic effort by Japanese diplomats to push neoliberal norms in Asia in order to counter China's rising influence.[38] Korea's Lee Myung Bak has also emphasized Korea's important role as an example that universal values and Asian values are not incompatible. India's prime minister, Manmohan Singh, has said that the entire world should follow the example of India, "an inclusive and open society, a multi-cultural, multi-ethnic, multi-lingual society."[39] And as Indonesians successfully participated in their second direct presidential election this summer, their government and parliament were urging ASEAN to pressure Burma and activate the human rights commission promised in the new ASEAN charter. To be sure, each of these nations has a different view of sovereignty and how democracy should be promoted, but they serve as powerful counterweights to any authoritarian model of government in Asia.

It is also an open question whether China's economy, let alone China's political system, will emerge stronger from the current financial crisis. Certainly, China's growth rates are more impressive than those of the United States or other Western democracies at this point. However, Beijing's current strategy of growth at the expense of all else is deepening the challenges of corruption, environmental degradation, rigid exchange rate policies, and dependence on external consumers. Moreover, the Chinese Communist Party may be more vulnerable to sustained economic retraction because its legitimacy as both a party and a system is tied closely to economic performance, whereas political parties in democracies may lose power because of the financial crisis without destroying the political system as a whole.[40]

The problem therefore may not be the attraction of the Chinese authoritarian political system itself, but rather the degree to which Beijing's economic expansion and adherence to mercantilist principles of "non-interference in internal affairs" undermines governance and enables dictators in problematic states like Burma or Sudan, or reversals of democracy in states like Thailand. As was noted earlier in the chapter, the other problem could lie in the impact of the financial crisis on China's convergence with the global economy and the danger (though unlikely at this point) of a replay of the Taisho Japan experience if there is a backlash against convergence and a turn to Chinese or Russian versions of "renovationism," protectionism, and autarky.

In general, the influence of authoritarian powers like China and Russia on democratic norms and governance in surrounding states is mixed, at best. If the economic crisis deepens and weaker democracies are put at risk, the role of the United States and more powerful democracies within those regions will have to increase.

Putting Democracy Back into U.S. Strategy

The promotion and support of democratic norms, human rights, and good governance has long been a central goal of U.S. foreign policy. Most U.S. administrations have recognized that advancing American values in these areas reinforces security. However, the Obama administration has been sending mixed signals about whether this is still seen as true in the wake of the Iraq War and the financial crisis. On China, the administration has suggested (perhaps inadvertently) that a softer tone on human rights was linked to American dependence on Beijing's purchases of Treasury notes. The muted response to China's crackdown in Xinjiang only reinforced this impression. In the Middle East, the relativism of the president's Cairo speech and the slow response to events in Tehran suggested that engagement strategies now trump concerns about fostering better governance and accountability in the region. This also appeared to be a subtext in Latin America, where the administration's low-key response to Venezuela's internal coup against the mayor of Caracas stood in contrast to a much firmer response to the military coup in Honduras. On the other hand, the president's speech in Accra on the importance of governance and accountability in Africa was masterful. It is not clear (at least to this observer) whether the difference in those approaches reflects different regional strategies, or whether the administration is still finding its footing on issues of human rights, democracy, and governance. If it is the latter, then the Accra speech suggests the trend is in the right direction.

It is important for the administration to put democracy back into its foreign policy strategy, particularly because of the current financial crisis. Theory and history suggest that a prolongation of the financial crisis could present us with more challenges (and possibly a few opportunities) with respect to the health of democracy worldwide. The United States and like-minded states need to continually check the pulse of democracies at risk and take collective action to shore up their domestic institutions and guard against reversals. Weaker governance around the world would only increase the dangers of future financial crises, and an international loss of confidence in democratic norms would undermine the stability of the neoliberal order and the hopes of millions.

Michael Green is concurrently a Senior Adviser and holds the Japan Chair at the Center for Strategic and International Studies and an associate professor of international relations at Georgetown University. Previously, he served as Special Assistant to the President for National Security Affairs and Senior Director for Asian Affairs at the National Security Council (NSC), from January 2004 to December 2005. Dr. Green joined the NSC in April 2001 as Director of Asian Affairs. From 1997 to 2000, he was Senior Fellow for Asian Security at the Council on Foreign Affairs. Dr. Green served as Senior Adviser to the Office of Asian Pacific Affairs at the Department of Defense in 1997 and as a consultant in the same office until 2000. From 1995 to 1997, he was a research staff member at the Institute for Defense Analyses, and from 1994 to 1995, an assistant professor of Asian studies at the Johns Hopkins University School of Advanced International Studies, where he remained a professorial lecturer until 2001. Dr. Green speaks fluent Japanese and spent over five years in Japan working as a staff member of the National Diet, as a journalist for Japanese and American newspapers, and as a consultant for U.S. businesses. He is Vice Chair of the congressionally mandated Japan-U.S. Friendship Commission and serves on the advisory boards of the Center for a New American Security and Australian American Leadership dialogue, and is a member of the editorial board of the *Washington Quarterly*. Dr. Green graduated from Kenyon College with highest honors in History and received an M.A. and Ph.D. from The Johns Hopkins School of Advanced International Studies. He was a Fulbright Fellow at Tokyo University and Research Associate with the MIT-Japan Program. He is a member of the Aspen Strategy Group.

[1] The author would like to thank CSIS Japan Chair summer interns Anna Lee, Lara Crouch, John Dougherty and Miko Oyama for their excellent assistance with research for this paper. The author also received invaluable insights from Peter Green, Erik Jensen and Eileen Pennington.

[2] Seymour Martin Lipset, "Some Social Requisites of Democracy," *American Political Science Review*, 53, no.1 (March 1959): 69-105.

[3] Lipset turns back to Aristotle to make his case, noting that "from Aristotle down to the present, men have argued that only in a wealthy society in which relatively few citizens lived in real poverty could a situation exist in which the mass of the population could intelligently participate in politics and could develop the self-restraint necessary to avoid succumbing to the appeals of irresponsible demagogues." Lipset, "Some Social Requisites of Democracy,"75.

[4] Michael Mandelbaum, "Democracy without America," *Foreign Affairs*, 86, no. 5 (September/October 2007): 119-130.

[5] Ronald Inglehart and Christian Welzel, "How Development Leads to Democracy," *Foreign Affairs*, 88, no. 2 (March/April 2009): 33-48.

[6] James Robinson, "Economic Development and Democracy," *Annual Review of Political Science*, 9 (2006): 503-527.

[7] Evelyn Huber, Dietrich Rueschemeyer and John Stephens, "The Impact of Economic Development on Democracy," *Journal of Economic Perspectives*, 7, no. 2 (Summer 1993): 71-86.

[8] Francis Fukuyama, "Democracy in U.S. Security Strategy," Center for Strategic and International Studies (April 2009).

[9] Ibid.

[10] Adam Przeworski and Fernando Limongi, "Modernization: Theories and Facts," *World Politics*, 49, no. 2 (January 1997): 155-183. Przeworski and Limongi were then challenged by Carlos Boix and Susan Stokes who purported to show through simulations that economic development was endogenous to democratization, and so the debate continues. See Boix and Stokes, "Endogenous Democratization," *World Politics*, 55, no. 4 (July 2003): 518-549.

[11] Ethan Kapstein and Nathan Converse, "Why Democracies Fail," *Journal of Democracy*, 19, no. 4 (October 2008): 57-68.

[12] Marc F. Plattner, "Why Authoritarian Economies Could Have More to Fear from the Crisis," *Washington Post*, 13 January 2009, Section A..

[13] Hugh Patrick, "The Economic Muddle of the 1920s," in James W. Morley, ed., *Dilemmas of Growth in Prewar Japan* (Princeton: Princeton University Press, 1971), 213.

[14] Jack Snyder, *Myths of Empire: Domestic Politics and International Ambition* (Ithaca, NY: Cornell University

Press, 1991). There is, of course, much more that can be said about Japan's return to the gold standard. Hugh Patrick and David Asher have pointed out, for example, that the problem was not the gold standard itself, but rather the failure of Japan to allow free market principles to operate effectively. See Hugh Patrick and David L. Asher, "Convergence and its Costs: The Failure of Japanese Economic Reform and the Breakdown of the Washington System, 1918-1932." PhD diss., St. Antony's College, Trinity, 2002.

[15] A.J.P. Taylor, *The Courses of German History* (New York: Paragaon Books, 1946), 189.

[16] "The LDC Debt Crisis," in *History of the Eighties: Lessons for the Future, Vol I: An Examination of the Banking Crises of the 1980s and Early 1990s* (Washington, D.C.: Federal Deposit Insurance Corporation, 1997), available at http://www.fdic.gov/bank/historical/history/191_210.pdf. By 1978, outstanding debt had increased to $159 billion.

[17] Jeffrey A. Frieden, *Global Capitalism* (New York: W.W. Norton, 2006), 374.

[18] Peter G. Snow and Luigi Manzetti, *Political Forces in Argentina* (Westport, CT: Praeger, 1993) and Raul Alfonsin, "The Transition toward Democracy in a Developing Country: The Case of Argentina" in *After Authoritarianism: Democracy or Disorder?*, ed. Daniel N. Nelson (Westport, CT: Praeger, 1995), 17-30.

[19] Francis Fukuyama, "The Latin American Experience," *Journal of Democracy* 19, no. 4 (October 2008).

[20] International Monetary Fund Fact Sheet, available at http://www.imf.org/External/np/exr/facts/asia.htm.

[21] United Nations Development Program, "Indonesia Human Development Report 2001," UNDP, 2001, 35.

[22] Asep Suryahadi, Sudarno Sumarto and Lant Pritchett, "Evolution of Poverty During the Crisis in Indonesia," *Asian Economic Journal*, 17, no. 3 (September 2003), 221-241.

[23] Stephan Haggard, *The Political Economy of the Asian Financial Crisis* (Washington, D.C.: Institute for International Economics, 2000), 2 and Chaibong Hahm, "South Korea's Miraculous Democracy," *Journal of Democracy*, 19, no. 3 (July 2008).

[24] According to country reports by *The Economist*, Thailand and the Philippines will contract by 4.4 percent and 1.8 percent in 2009, respectively. The reports are available at http://countryanalysis.eiu.com/country_reports

[25] Although China has positive GDP growth projections in 2009 despite the economic crisis, its export growth rate was -22.4 percent this year, compared with 17.1 percent last year. Vietnam is also projected to eke out positive growth this year, but its exports are also doing poorly because of its significant economic ties to struggling countries such as the United States, Japan, and EU countries. Sources: http://edc.ca/english/docs/gchina_e.pdf; http://www.eai.nus.edu.sg/BB447.pdf

[26] Roger Altman, "Globalization in Retreat," *Foreign Affairs*, 88, no. 4 (July/August 2009), 2-8.

[27] Ibid.

[28] World Bank Development Indicators Database, available at http://web.worldbank.org/WBSITE/EXTERNAL/DATASTATISTICS/0,,contentMDK:20535285~menuPK:1192694~pagePK:64133150~piPK:64133175~theSitePK:239419,00.html.

[29] See http://www.nationmaster.com/graph/eco_for_dir_inv_net_inf_of_gdp-direct-investment-net-inflows-gdp. Source listed as World Bank Development Indicator's Database.

[30] "Iran Country Report," Development Data Group (DECDG), World Bank, 27 March 2009. Data on China and Vietnam obtained from the World Bank Development Indicators Database.

[31] Azar Gat, "The Return of Authoritarian Great Powers," *Foreign Affairs*, 86, no. 4 (July/August 2007), 59-69 and Robert Kagan, *The Return of History and the End of Dreams* (New York: Knopf, 2008).

[32] Joshua Kurlantzick, *Charm Offensive: How China's Soft Power is Transforming the World* (New Haven: Yale University Press, 2007) and David Kang, *China Rising: Peace, Power, and Order in East Asia* (New York: Columbia University Press, 2007).

[33] Roger Altman, "Globalization in Retreat," *Foreign Affairs*, 88, no. 4 (July/August 2009), 2-8.

[34] "Soft Power in Asia," Chicago Council on Global Affairs (2008).

[35] As reported in Doh Chull Shin, "Democratization in East Asia: A Cultural Perspective," Working paper (14 April 14 2009).

[36] Bates Gill et al., "Strategic Views on Asian Regionalism," Center for Strategic and International Studies (February 2009).

[37] Melissa Murphy, "Decoding Chinese Politics: Intellectual Debates and Why They Matter," Center for Strategic and International Studies (January 2008).

[38] See, for example: Junichiro Koizumi, "Japan and ASEAN in East Asia – A Sincere and Open Partnership" (speech, Singapore, 14 January 14 2002) available at http://www.kantei.go.jp/foreign/koizumispeech/2002/01/14speech_e.html and "The Joint Ministerial Statement of the Initiative for Development of East Asia," (official communiqué issued at the close of the ASEAN summit, Tokyo, Japan, 12 August 12 2002); Junichiro Koizumi, "Speech by H.E. Mr. Junichiro Koizumi, Prime Minister of Japan" (keynote speech, Asia-Africa Business Summit, Jakarta, Indonesia, 22 April 2005), available at http://www.kantei.go.jp/foreign/koizumispeech/2005/04/22speech_e.html; Foreign Minister Taro Aso, "Asian Strategy as I See it: Japan as the Thought Leader of Asia" (speech, Foreign Correspondents' Club, Tokyo, Japan, 7 December 7 2005), available at http://www.mofa.go.jp/announc/fm/aso/speech0512; Taro Aso, "Policy Speech by Minister for Foreign Affairs Taro Aso to the 166th Session of the Diet" (speech, Tokyo, Japan, 26 January 2007); Taro Aso, "On the Arc of Freedom and Prosperity" (keynote address, Japan Forum for International Relations, International House of Japan, Tokyo, Japan, 12 March 2007); Shinzo Abe, "Toward Further Collaboration" (speech, North Atlantic Council on Japan and NATO, Brussels, Belgium, 12 January 2007); "Joint Statement by Japan and the Republic of India on the Enhancement of Cooperation on Environmental Protection and Energy Security," (official communiqué, New Delhi, India, 22 August 2007) available at http://www.mofa.go.jp/region/asia-paci/pmv0708/joint-3.html.

[39] The transcript of Prime Minister Singh's remarks at the India Today Conclave, New Delhi, 25 February 2005 is available at http//www.pmindia.nic.in/speeches.htm (cited in C. Raja Mohan, *Impossible Allies: Nuclear India United States and the Global Order* (Delhi: India Research Press, 2006), 93.

[40] Plattner, "Why Authoritarian Economies Could Have More to Fear from the Crisis."

Part 5

CONCLUDING OBSERVATIONS

CHAPTER 10

Summary of the Aspen Strategy Group Deliberations

Nicholas Burns
Director, Aspen Strategy Group
Professor of the Practice of Diplomacy and International Politics
Harvard University

Summary of the Aspen Strategy Group Deliberations on the Economic Crisis and its Implications for Foreign Policy and National Security

Nicholas Burns
Director
Aspen Strategy Group

From July 31 to August 5, 2009, the Aspen Strategy group met for its annual summer session to consider the consequences and challenges the global economic crisis poses for America's national security. Over the last twelve months the world has seen the fall of governments, the collapse of Lehman Brothers, an implosion on Wall Street, global bail-outs and stimulus packages, rising unemployment, and depressed growth in the developed and developing world.

What will happen over the next twelve months? Will the economic crisis in the developing world cause rising political instability? Will we see more shifts in the balance of power and more governments fail? Has America's reputation been severely weakened by this crisis? What other implications does this crisis portend for America's national security?

These are some of the questions we asked our authors to explore in the preceding papers, and were the critical items for discussion facing the group in Aspen. Several key observations and topics of concern dominated our discussions.

The Concerns

I. Prospects for a Global Power Shift

The most important strategic question posed during the Aspen Strategy Group's deliberations was whether, as Robert Blackwill asked, the world economic crisis would lead to a major shift in the global balance of power as occurred after the

Napoleonic Wars, the First and Second World Wars and during the end of the Cold War.

Most agreed that the answer to that extraordinarily important question depends on two factors—the length and severity of the crisis and the possibility of catastrophic events affecting the leading powers—that are simply unknowable at this time. As Blackwill pointed out, there has already been substantial turbulence caused by the crisis, including the fall of the Latvian and Icelandic governments, riots in Greece, and social turbulence in Africa, Asia, and the Middle East. But we have not seen the kind of catastrophic events produced by the economic crisis that could alter the global balance of power in the near term. At the present time, it does not appear that the economic crisis will lead to radical change in the international system.

II. Predictions on American Decline

A second, critical question we asked was whether the economic crisis will lead to the eventual erosion of U.S. global dominance. Many participants noted that the credibility of the U.S. as global leader was damaged significantly by the economic crisis and by earlier mistakes such as the failed recovery effort after Hurricane Katrina. Some members predicted that the U.S. will remain the leading economic, military, and political power for decades; while others argued that China's gross domestic product might overtake that of the U.S. by 2025, allowing China to challenge the United States in other spheres of power. Questions also remain regarding whether China itself would be buffeted by political instability, income inequality, and regional problems that might retard its own growth and prevent it from challenging the U.S. for world economic power in the decades ahead.

Still, many participants concluded that American society and the U.S. economy remain resilient. We have strengths in many leading edge industries. The dollar and the U.S. Treasury market will likely go unchallenged in the short term. The U.S. will remain the major thought leader in international economic circles for the future.

III. Prognosis for Recovery

Charting the course of the economic crisis for the end of 2009 and beginning of 2010 is vital to global recovery. While many pointed to signs that the recovery is already underway, some of the economists present at our meeting in Aspen cautioned that the recession could possibly grow worse before it abated, that we may see more bank failures, and that the United States would have to adapt to lower global and U.S. growth rates for some time. Moreover, some reminded us that the early signs of a recovery could be illusory and America could possibly suffer a downward shift in its economic fortunes.

We focused on global trade as an important factor in the economic recovery. Some commented that it is striking that President Obama has not revealed a coherent strategy on trade eight months into his presidency. In Washington, support in the U.S. for free trade and free trade agreements has diminished, and there is a lack of consensus in the U.S. concerning the future of the Doha Round of the world trade talks, planned free trade agreements with South Korea and Colombia, and dual-use export restrictions.

IV. Prospective Consequences

Some participants argued that European countries, in particular, could face a banking crisis and declining growth that might have negative consequences for NATO military budgets and thus for allied effectiveness in Afghanistan. Pakistan and Ukraine are also possible, notable victims of the economic crisis. Another key problem was that the youth of the world, having from 2002 to 2007 experienced some of the best five years in recent global economic history, might be profoundly disillusioned with a prolonged period of recession. There could be tangible consequences for the world as a whole—a decline in trade and private capital flows and remittances, lower growth and productivity, and higher unemployment.

Suggestions for the Days Ahead

V. Domestic Reform Should Precede International Structural Change

Some Aspen members expressed concern about the impact on the economy of "chemotherapy after the crisis." Others suggested opposition to President Obama's economic agenda within the business community. Participants asked whether President Obama and the Democratic majority in Congress can achieve the right balance in regulatory reform? Most agreed that it is important for the U.S. to achieve major, structural reforms at home in health, education, and regulation of financial markets as a prerequisite for a full international recovery.

VI. Options for International Structural Reform

We spent significant time and energy in Aspen discussing the future of global governance. Some pointed out the irony of the U.S. as simultaneously a leader of global governance and also one of its major skeptics. A pressing concern is the trade-off between the legitimacy and effectiveness of major international institutions. Now that the G-8 has been largely retired in favor of the G-20, will it lead to reform of other major international political institutions such as the United Nations, IMF, and World Bank?

Some argued that the U.S. should be more ambitious and consider a major overhaul of the international system as another generation of global leaders did so impressively following the Second World War. Others argued that we should reform the system currently in existence, rather than seek to create new institutions. One participant said: "don't start over in a historic preservation district. Renovate from the inside."

We agreed that it remains to be seen how ambitious the Obama administration will be in seeking major changes in the international system.

VII. A Necessary Rebalancing at Home, and Abroad

A particularly vital question that we asked in the face of all these challenges and responsibilities: Is the global community capable of tackling effectively the huge challenges before us—climate change, the threat of pandemics, terrorism, nuclear proliferation, possible world food shortages, and poverty?

At home, the ability of the United States government to respond effectively to these and other challenges must be carefully examined. This is a time of real testing for the U.S. authorities. Our institutions sometimes seem, in the word of one of our members, "overmatched" by the crisis. Several questions arose from the group during this discussion. Does the U.S. government have a sufficient number of people in the Treasury and other agencies to deal with the market crisis? Is coordination among the agencies sufficiently effective? Will the president and other senior officials treat the Treasury on a par with the Defense and State Departments as a critical actor in our national security? Has the new administration made the necessary internal reforms to reflect the fact that the economy is now the most important issue facing our country? If so, why does the State Department persist in calling attention to its mantra, "Defense, Diplomacy and Development" with no mention of the primacy of economics in our national security decision-making?

VIII. Remedies for the Impact on Development and Democracy

We agreed that the current crisis has had a highly negative impact in the developing world, in particular, with a massive drop in capital flows, remittances, and jobs. One participant remarked that fragile states have been hit particularly hard with a risk to their neighbors from refugees, drugs, and terrorism. Most agreed that Afghanistan and Pakistan are a crucial test for the efficacy of development assistance and there is an urgent need to agree upon a more effective framework in those countries for assistance, development, and counterinsurgency.

The group agreed that the U.S. should seek better international coordination of aid to redress global imbalances. But, it is unclear how ambitious President Obama can and will be. Eight months after his inauguration, a USAID administrator had yet to be named. We debated, at a time of budget stringency, if Congress should obligate funds necessary to rebuild USAID and bolster the Foreign Assistance budget. The requirements are numerous, including strengthening the Foreign Service by funding hundreds of new positions and the development needs that may be required by a prolonged Afghan war. To fill in these gaps, the value of public-private partnerships and the positive impact of U.S. foreign investment by the private sector must be better utilized.

Another major question is the impact of the crisis on democratic states and the democratic system as a whole. The U.S. and others must consider how to protect vulnerable democracies in Eastern Europe during this crisis and should keep a watchful eye to ensure the democratic system remains strong.

IX. Debating America's Global Leadership Role

Perhaps most important—and hardest to define—are the wider questions raised by the economic crisis that go to the heart of America's global leadership. Will the rest of the world recover some of the confidence clearly lost in U.S. global leadership? Will the American public and Congress continue to support a leading international role for the U.S.? The latter is a particularly difficult question to answer, given domestic pressures against foreign aid, the controversy over outsourcing, disagreements on trade, and the loss of jobs at home. We must better understand this nexus between our domestic environment and foreign policy needs. Though a series of unforeseen events could return some of our political leaders to a semi-isolationist stance, many of us are optimistic that the U.S. is returning to international favor due in part, to President Obama's engaged international leadership.

As we are a non-partisan group, we all wish President Obama, his administration, and Congress well as they seek to promote the leadership role of the U.S. that remains at the heart of our foreign policy.